T0220286

Planning, Negotiating, Implementing, and Managing Wide Area Networks

Luiz Augusto de Carvalho and Benjamin Naude

iUniverse, Inc.
New York Bloomington

iUniverse books may be ordered through booksellers or by contacting:

iUniverse
1663 Liberty Drive
Bloomington, IN 47403
www.iuniverse.com
1-800-Authors (1-800-288-4677)

Because of the dynamic nature of the Internet, any Web addresses or links contained in this book may have changed since publication and may no longer be valid. The views expressed in this work are solely those of the author and do not necessarily reflect the views of the publisher, and the publisher hereby disclaims any responsibility for them.

ISBN: 978-1-4401-6390-6 (sc)
ISBN: 978-1-4401-6391-3 (hc)
ISBN: 978-1-4401-6423-1 (ebook)

Library of Congress Control Number: 2009936150

Printed in the United States of America

iUniverse rev. date: 09/14/09

Contents

Preface

Our objective is to transmit our work experience in planning and implementing wide area networks (WANs) in the last twenty years. Literature is lacking in this area of expertise. The lessons that professionals in the field learn are rarely documented and shared. Additionally, there is a tendency to focus on technical aspects negatively affecting planning and managing aspects in the available literature.

Another motivating factor is the gap between the people studying algorithms in the universities and the professionals in the field of planning and operating the large WANs. We intend to reduce this gap, showing how those resources (algorithms) can be effectively applied. This book will provide a general view about how WANs should be planned, priced, negotiated, and managed. We do not intend to discuss aspects linked to the technical management of large WANs, given the fact that there is already much literature on this subject.

The target audience of this book is IT managers and telecommunications managers of medium- and large-sized organizations. We assume the reader has some basic understanding of both the technical aspects of WAN management and the broader subject this book describes, including basic financial principles.

Each chapter targets a different aspect of the planning, implementation, and management of WANs. Each can be read individually to meet specific needs. In chapter one, we explain, from our point of view, what constitutes a telecommunications network. Subsequently, in chapter two, we define the concepts and terminologies adopted throughout this book. We strongly suggest you read these chapters, even if you intend to read the following ones piecemeal.

1

General View of What Constitutes Telecommunication Networks

Telecommunications networks are logistics systems. What sets telecommunications networks apart from traditional materials logistics systems is the fact that instead of transporting loads, we transport data, voice, and images. So the same concepts applicable to planning logistic networks are applicable to planning telecommunications networks. Making a direct analogy:

- The data packets are the loads.
- The users are the senders and receivers of the loads.
- The aggregation nodes are the warehouses.
- The several transportation means (airplane, ships, trucks, and so forth) are the transport technologies (frame relay, MPLS, X.25, and so forth).The several transport companies are the service providers.

The understanding of this analogy is fundamental to the understanding of several concepts discussed throughout this book.

Another important concept is that, from a macro perspective, there is only one large telecommunications network in the world (as only one large logistic system), and the service providers can own parts of this network or just use it.[1] The system was thought to allow a packet delivered in a segment to be transported through

---

1   This is similar to a railway company that owns its tracks and a truck company that just uses the public highways.

several subsegments until it got to its final destination. Extending the logistic system concept, there are basically three types of arrangements:

- National telecommunications infrastructures where the ownership is public and the service providers just use the means (for example, highways)
- Infrastructures owned by the service providers (analogous to railways)
- Transport systems where there is no need for building means but just the regulation of the available space and building the embarkation points (for example, maritime and air transportation)

Of course, the network as a whole encompasses a mix of these alternatives. As we can see, the telecommunications infrastructure has an almost-perfect analogy to a transportation infrastructure. So a large organization should see its telecommunications network as a subset of this logistical system (worldwide public network). The understanding of this concept, although seemingly academic, is very important to allow the telecommunications managers to evaluate and put issues like transport costs and deployment of specific technologies in perspective.

As mentioned, when discussing transport alternatives for voice and data traffic, the issues involved are *mutatis mutandis*, the same ones involved when discussing alternatives to a typical logistic network. The issues are as follows:

- How much does it cost to transport a kilobyte of data?
- How reliable is the delivery process?
- How fast can it be delivered?
- What value-added services are included?
- Can I trace my packets and check what happened to them?
- How much leverage do I have over the service provider?
- If I had my own network, would it be cheaper?
- From where and to where will my cargo flow?
- What is the distribution of my flow over time?

As we can see, these questions have to be answered both in a logistic network and a telecommunications network. Another important concept to be defined is our understanding of the difference between private and a public networks.

A public network is a structure that several users and organizations use without any particular association among them. A public network need not be composed of only one technology or provider. A public network can encompass several different physical means that are subcontracted from several service providers.

On the other hand, the objective of a private network is to provide connectivity only for a particular group of users belonging to a specific organization. Note that a private network can use several public networks to provide connectivity or use its own infrastructure (optical fiber, radio links, and so forth). This book's focus is in planning, managing, and implementing private networks, although most concepts are applicable to both public and private.

The primary goal of the management of a private network is to guarantee connectivity to the organization with the desired quality of service for the least cost. So cost management is a fundamental part of managing telecommunications networks. Traditionally, five main strategies keep the telecommunications cost down:

- Pressure the service providers and hardware vendors while trying to guarantee low prices (for example, bargaining and negotiating hard)
- Enhance the internal control over usage of the services available (for example, billing systems, classes of restrictions, and restricting Web accesses)
- Increase the control over the service providers to ensure the organization is paying only for what was really used at the agreed value for each service (for example, telephone bills auditing)
- Try to reduce costs with the workforce through outsourcing
- Carefully craft network designs

Carefully crafting network designs using algorithms, however, is a much more effective way of achieving savings. Doing that makes it possible to establish the optimal correlation between the organization's geographical dispersion, its traffic volumes/flows, and the tariff system. This view:

- Makes possible the understanding of the trade-offs between cost, performance, and reliability
- Allows a proper negotiation with the service providers
- Tends to produce lasting savings

Getting the design right is important. Overengineering an overpriced network does not require tools or elaborate processes. The true challenge lies in the design of an optimal structure, which minimizes cost while maximizing performance. To achieve this objective while executing all necessary calculations manually is virtually impossible. That's why the deployment of design tools is so important. The magnitude of the savings achievable using this strategy of redesigning the network varies and is directly related to the size and geographical dispersion of the organization's sites.

In addition, the same process used to carefully craft the network design can also assist in several other aspects associated with contracting, pricing, and managing a WAN/telecommunications infrastructure. These include activities that:

- Evaluate service providers' bids, fairly comparing different kinds of services, technologies, and pricing strategies
- Evaluate how much would be fair to pay to outsource a network
- Analyze the current WAN, comparing it with the several interconnection alternatives available throughout the market (benchmarking)
- Validate the deployment of technologies such as VSAT, MPLS, frame relay, and VPN
- Evaluate the feasibility of integrating voice and data using different strategies and technologies (for example, integration total or partial using VoIP, Voframe, or VoATM)

- Negotiate telecommunication budgets establishing a clear correlation between traffic, quality of service (QoS), and cost
- Simulate future needs and verify how the network's cost will behave faced with increase in traffic (assist in strategic planning and anticipate needs and problems)
- Analyze traffic and check if the number of trunks, bandwidth allocation, and committed information rate (CIR) definitions are adequate (capacity planning)

Careful planning of the target infrastructure provides four specific benefits:

- Makes it possible to compare the planned with the actual cost of the network
- Makes it possible to identify what needs to be implemented and/or changed and set the whole project plan, including phases and schedules
- Makes clear which cost factors in the actual structure could be reduced
- Makes possible to produce a very straightforward, high-level management report comparing the actual expenditures with the proposed ones
- Shows the necessary investments and potential savings and return over investment (ROI) of the project calculated

Those analyses are crucial when looking for funding. In addition, careful planning of the network design makes it possible to properly analyze alternatives such as outsourcing or external management. Knowing the cost to build an optimized structure better position an evaluation of cost benefits of various outsourced solutions.

Although the identification of an ideal structure to support a given traffic volume is a huge benefit in itself, the ability to calculate these structures quickly allows the organization to perform many calculations using several traffic volumes and establish the correlation between volume and cost. Such calculation allows the organization to project the growth of the traffic, verifying not only how much the network could be costing today but also how much it would cost if the traffic increases by a given rate.

Logistical systems, like telecommunications networks, demand good planning to be effective, and this planning is usually too complex to be done manually, even in a medium-sized network.

2

Entities and Concepts Involved in a Telecommunications Network

To clarify the concepts and terminologies adopted in this book, we are defining the entities involved with a telecommunications network. The understanding of these concepts will allow a better understanding of the subsequent topics. Here it is interesting to notice that, although most of these concepts may sound extremely simple and even obvious, when combined they may not be. In addition, we must understand them well enough to be able to recognize them in projects and problems where the nomenclature is completely distinct. We divide these entities into three types: functional, technical, and structural.

2.1 Functional

Functional entities are associated with the network but not components of the network itself. We identified eight entities that we classify as functional:

- **Organization:** The entire corporation, group, or other association that the WAN is connecting. The organization also encompasses the business units. A practical understanding of what that means can be visualized if we think about a state government as the organization and its several departments and state companies as its business units. The same concept can be applied to a large multinational corporation where its several country operations/business segments can be considered as independent business units.

- **Business unit:** A subset of an organization whose criteria for segmentation can be multifold (geographical, type of activity conducted, and so forth).
- **Address:** A physical location touched by the organization's network.
- **Point of presence (POP):** The physical location of the business units. (An address can have more than one POP located there.)
- **Service provider:** The company providing telecommunications services for the organization.
- **Contract:** The agreement between the organizations/business units and the service providers. It also has a price list associated with it.
- **Price list:** Each contract has its associated price list where the values to be charged are described.
- **Request:** Interaction between the organizations/business units and service providers. The organization can request maintenance, new telecommunications resources, changes in the existing ones, or cancel resources.

The relationships among the entities described are as follows:

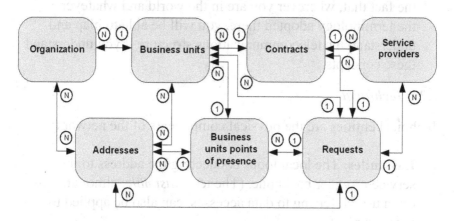

- One organization can have several business units.
- One business unit belongs to only one organization but can be present in several addresses (POPs).
- An address can host several POPs belonging to several business units.
- A POP belongs to only one business unit and is located in only one address.
- A business unit can have several contracts with several service provides.
- A business unit can make several requests to several service providers.
- A service provider can have several contracts with several business units.
- A service provider can provide several connections for several organizations/business units.
- A contract can belong to only one service provider.
- A contract belongs to only one organization.
- A contract can serve several business units of the same organization.
- A request is linked to only one contract although we can have several requests associated with one contract.
- A request is always associated with only one equipment, last mile, or connection.

- Understanding the functional entities is very important given the fact that, wherever you are in the world and whatever the terminology adopted there, you will be able to map and understand the telecommunications structure if you understand these concepts.

2.2 Technical

Technical entities are the physical components of the network:

- **Last miles:** The local loops connecting the address to the service provider backbone. (The term *last mile*, although most often used referring to data accesses, can also be applied to voice trunks.)
- **Equipment/Customer-premises equipment (CPE):** Connected to the end of the last mile.
- **Cloud:** Does not constitute a real entity and is a simplification of the service provider infrastructure. The use of this simplification is necessary when conceptually analyzing a private network where the resources subcontracted to a service provider can be grouped and called "cloud."
- **Connections:** Connections between two physical locations (dedicated or switched). They are composed of the elements: equipment A, last mile A, backbone, last mile B, equipment B, and so forth.[2]
- The following picture represents the relationship among these elements.

---

2   The use of A to B terms does not mean any directional bias. The connections usually flow in both ways.

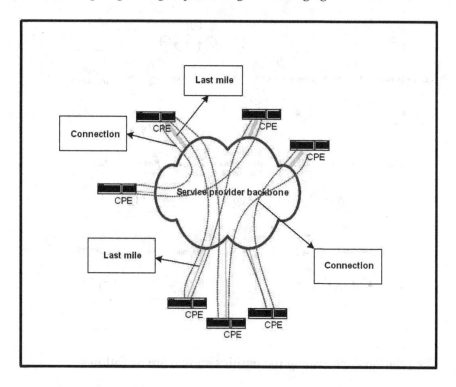

As we can see in the picture above, a connection between any given location A and any other location B is composed of the elements:

- **End A equipment:** With or without an associated port (CPE A)
- **End A last mile:** The local loop between the address A and the service provider backbone (represented as a cloud)
- **Service provider backbone:** Represented as a cloud
- **End B last mile:** The local loop between the address B and the service provider backbone (represented as a cloud)
- **End B equipment:** With or without an associated port (CPE B)
- **Connection between A and B:** A composition of the other entities

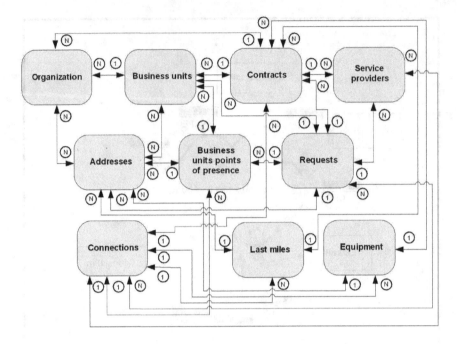

The relationships among the entities shown are as follows:

- A service provider can have several contracts, each one with several connections.
- A contract can include more than one last mile.
- A contract can include more than one equipment.
- A connection can be composed by last miles and equipment belonging to different contracts/service providers.
- A last mile belongs to only one contract.
- A last mile can be used by several connections.
- A last mile connects the service provider backbone to only one address.
- An equipment belongs to only one contract.
- An equipment can be used by more than one connection.
- An equipment is located at only one physical address.
- A connection is usually associated with one service provider but can be associated with at maximum five (equipment A, last mile A, backbone, last mile B, and equipment B).
- A connection has only one equipment and last mile associated with each one of its ends.

- A connection is associated with only one POP (and address) in each one of its ends.

Different connections can share equipment and a last mile. It is not uncommon to have equipment and last miles with one, two, three, or more connections. Each connection though is associated with only one equipment and last mile in each one of its ends.

The elements that every connection encompasses (equipment A, last mile A, backbone, last mile B, equipment B, and the connection itself) are cost factors. Depending on the pricing strategy that the service provider adopted, some of these cost factors may seem to be zero for a specific connection. However, conceptually speaking, every connection has these cost factors associated with the technical entities. Some of these may be shared by more than one connection. In which case, a portion of the costs must be allocated to each connection to accurately determine costs. For more information about calculating costs, see chapter four. For clarification, connections are entities representing throughput between two points. Throughput has two basic attributes:

- **Minimum guaranteed flow:** Usually in packet networks referred to as CIR
- **Maximum possible flow:** Usually in packet networks referred to as extended information rate (EIR)

This concept is not linked to the technology used to provide the connection. Our understanding is that the organization buys throughput among its POPs from the service providers. In the picture, we can see the entities which constitute a connection:

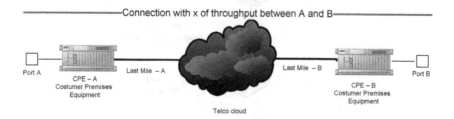

─────────────────Connection with x of throughput between A and B─────────────────

Port A · CPE – A Costumer Premises Equipment · Last Mile – A · Telco cloud · Last Mile – B · CPE – B Costumer Premises Equipment · Port B

Traffic is not shown. This represents only the basic conceptual model. The pricing strategy that the service provider adopted can be applied across this model, although some items may not have associated cost. We use this model to understand and consistently format the several pricing strategies to allow comparison and good decision-making. See chapter four for further discussion and examples.

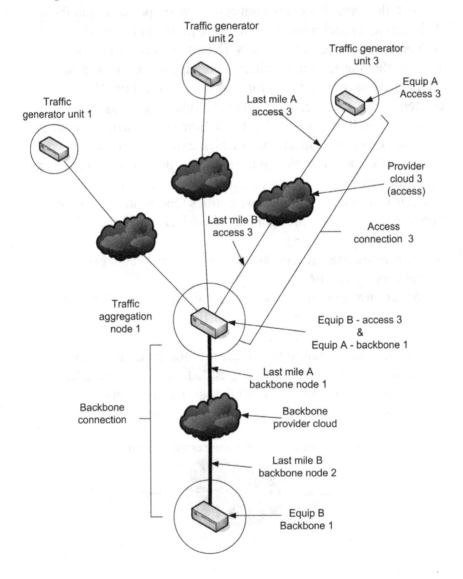

2.3 *Structural*

In addition to functional and technical entities, each network has structural entities. These are conceptually more difficult than the technical entities, but related to them. Picture 5 shows how the technical entities are articulated in a WAN, where the topology is not a star. This diagram is a bit more complicated than the one shown in picture 3. Here we have a situation where there are aggregation nodes and different service providers for the connections. In addition to that, we have connections linking the sites to the nodes (access) and connections linking the nodes between themselves (backbone). This picture helps us to become familiar with the entities, which we call structural:

- **Traffic generator unit:** A source or destination of traffic. In corporate networks, traffic generator units are usually workstations and people, although this may vary.
- **Traffic unit:** A group of traffic generator units. In corporate networks, traffic units are usually the organization's POPs.
- **Traffic aggregation node:** The point where, for transportation reasons, the traffic is aggregated before being distributed. Following an analogy with a logistic network, the nodes would be the warehouses where the goods are stored and from where they are distributed.
- **Backbone:** The connections between the traffic aggregation nodes.
- **Access:** The connections between the traffic units (sites) and traffic aggregation nodes (nodes).

Structural entities may be more complex than technical entities. Even though each connection has only one last mile at each end (although multiple connections can share the same last mile), some structural entities can overlap in more complicated ways. For example, a given location can be a traffic unit and traffic aggregation node at the same time. In which case, there is no separate connection that would be the access between the two.

The term *backbone* is not associated with the bandwidth, even though there is a tendency for the bandwidths of the backbone connections to be bigger.

Another important aspect, which is not always obvious, is the fact that equipment and last miles can be part of access and backbone connections. For example, equipment node 1 in picture 5 supports connections between nodes and between the node and sites.

Such concepts are applicable both to private and public networks (dedicated or switched). In this book, our focus is on private networks, so some concepts expressed may have their meaning slightly changed when applied to public networks. Because public networks may comprise units that have no association with one another, there would likely be less similarity between different traffic units within the network, for example.

The subsequent pictures illustrate how the traffic generator units are associated with the traffic units. The traffic generator units are the sources and destinations of traffic for the particular network. As we can see, in a pure data network, the traffic generator units are workstations and servers. In a pure voice network, the traffic generator units are people (phone extensions). In an integrated network, both types of traffic generator units exist.

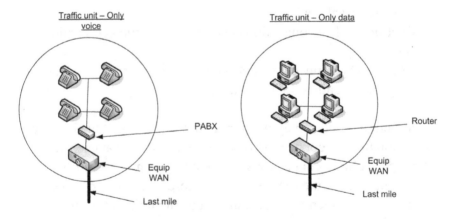

Traffic unit - voice and Data

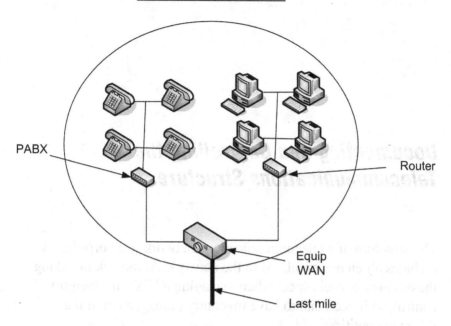

This chapter introduced the three types of entities associated with telecommunications networks: functional, technical, and structural. These concepts are the fundamentals for the discussions in this book.

3

Documenting and Controlling the Telecommunications Structure

The structure of a telecommunications network in a corporation includes all elements related to the network. At the risk of stating the obvious, a vital aspect when managing a WAN is inventory control, so it is crucial to have inventory management of the following entities:

- The organizations using the network
- The business units served by the network
- The physical locations touched by the network
- POPs of the business units in the physical locations
- Service providers
- The contracts with the price lists and items supported by each contract
- The equipment, including the rented and owned and their location and cost
- The last miles including capacity, location, and cost
- The dedicated connections being used, indicating the capacity and location of each end (A and B)
- The interactions with the service providers (every interaction must be formal)[3]
- The monthly cost of the infrastructure, including the expenses and depreciation

---

3　In this sense, interaction means each time anyone from the organization requests anything from the service providers.

The statement that the managers of the structure must have this information does not necessarily mean that they must have a particular system to control it. Such inventory can be held in spreadsheets or even in printed lists. A dedicated system makes this task easier, but, if procedures are in place to use and update simple lists, this usually is sufficient to the task. If a manager of a telecommunications network cannot provide this information quickly and accurately, he or she cannot effectively manage the network. The telecommunications manager may contract people to build the inventory for him or her and then just keep it updated. He or she may contract people to keep the inventory updated as well, or he or she may do both things internally with his or her own team. There is no miracle here. Whatever the strategy adopted, nothing related to telecommunications should be contracted without the knowledge of the telecommunications area. All changes, inclusions, and canceling of resources have to go through the telecommunications area. In this way, the inventory tends to be kept updated. The more common problem comes when the users have autonomy to request resources directly from the service providers. (The interactions are not centralized and informal.)

It is extremely common to find situations where the people who are supposed to manage the network do not have a complete view of the resources under their responsibility. In large multinational companies, it is very common for different groups within the organization to contract the structure. For example, headquarters contract part of the network, and local teams contract the other part. To add to this problem, it is very common to see different business units having autonomy to contract telecommunications resources, sometimes not even bothering to communicate to the people who are supposed to manage the whole structure. This often leads to situations when, due to either management failures or cultural/systemic situations, managers are not effectively executing their mandate. Here, we clearly perceive the importance of having a unified process to control the telecommunications resources in large multinational organizations.

The existence of a network operations center (NOC) and/ or monitoring tools do not guarantee by itself the existence of an adequate inventory of resources. Above all, it does not guarantee an adequate link between resources contracted and values expended (expenses or depreciation).

When replanning a telecommunications structure, it is not unusual to find savings. Frequently, organic growth causes the organization's structure to become inefficient, even if initial planning was well executed. Expansions of specific sites can make different structures or pricing agreements with service providers a better choice than the current plans. Replanning to respond to growth can therefore lead to significant savings. The connection alternatives and costs usually change since the last planning occurred. As a result, when we finally do a replanning of the whole structure, large savings are usually realized.

In the last chapters of this book, we are going to explain step-by-step how to plan (or replan) a WAN. The phases do not differ much from a typical engineering project. We divided the process into three main phases:

- Data gathering and understanding the needs (chapter fourteen)
- Generating the designs (chapter fifteen)
- Discussing the results and making adjustments (chapters sixteen and seventeen)

The process of documenting and controlling inventory discussed in this chapter will help the telecommunications manager know what current costs really are, determine the major cost drivers in the network, project what the costs of any changes will be, and control overall cost. One key to cost control is effective price negotiation with service providers. In the next several chapters, we are going to discuss the aspects linked with pricing and negotiating a WAN.

4

The Cost and the Price

When planning and implementing a WAN, the goal is to meet the connectivity requirements at the lowest total cost. So accurately setting the minimum quality and quantity requirements is paramount. This starting point should not include the technical details of the type of connections or equipment to be used because these are options to be considered. They are not basic connectivity needs. Although a lot of literature can be found discussing the advantages of using specific technologies and pros and cons of using each one of them, our view is that such discussions usually have an overly technical approach. Their emphasis is on features whose cost-benefit correlation is very difficult to measure. Such discussions when planning a WAN tend to take away the focus from the main issues associated with planning a WAN. Such focus has to be how to provide connectivity in the cheapest and safest way possible.

Discussing the kind of technology to deploy is similar to determining what type of transportation is the best: maritime, air, railways, or highways. This is an empty discussion if the volume and destinations of what we intend to transport and the costs associated and availability of routes are unclear. In a logistics network, destination often simply determines the mode of transportation. For example, railways are not available to ship goods from New York to Tokyo, but ships and airplanes are. Similarly, the amount of freight to be transported may make the determination between ships and airplanes. The telecommunications network transports data. The specific methods chosen will depend on the locations and amounts of traffic. Once details are known, the costs and benefits of each specific technology become measurable.

Heated debates have raged regarding the pros and cons of specific transport technologies. Concerns with the traffic mapping (volume, interest, and profile) and transport strategies rarely inspire such vigorous discussion. Yet these important considerations should take precedence in planning a WAN. The specific technology is subordinate to achievement of the final goal, connectivity of suitable quality, and quantity at the lowest achievable cost.

Although this definition of what should be the focus when planning and managing a WAN seems a bit obvious, our experience shows that, very often, the planning of these networks is executed by technical people whose mind-set tends to lead them to focus on technology. In addition, we have the part played by the hardware vendors and service providers influencing the buyers (the teams planning the network) who are selling features and technologies as benefits. Such context tends to take away the focus from mapping traffic (volume, interest, and profile) and comparing transport strategies. These aspects are sometimes completely bypassed.

Of course, an organization planning (or replanning) its WAN must consider a compound of factors including technological tendencies. However, never lose the focus on the main issues:

- What is the volume to be transported?
- What is the interest of traffic?
- What is the profile of the traffic?
- What transport strategies are available? What are the costs of each one of them?

Once again, the issue of the cost associated with a WAN has to be put in the context of a logistic network. The main question to be answered is, "What is the cheapest and safest way to transport my traffic (data, voice, and so forth)?"

Typically, we have a defined value plus a variable value associated with the volume. The cost model usually varies between the two extremes: entirely defined to entirely variable. We usually have cost models that include both fixed and variable costs. The results lie between these two extremes. Each connection has cost factors, including the technical entities introduced in chapter two (equipment at each end, last miles at each end, the backbone, and the connection itself). Depending on the pricing strategy that the service provider adopted, some of these cost factors may seem to be zero for a specific connection. It is, for example, possible that, in some cases, the organization owns the equipment. In these situations, this equipment still has a cost that is represented by the total cost of ownership (TCO). TCO includes the weighted average cost of capital (WACC) of the organization plus maintenance and management costs.

The idea is to identify the cost of providing connectivity between two defined points, A and B. Conceptually speaking, every connection has cost factors associated with the technical entities. The equipment and last miles costs are easily linked with the cost of providing connectivity between point A and B. However, more than one connection may sometimes share them. In which case, a portion of the costs must be allocated to each. The cost of the cloud is always shared by all connections, which makes it a bit more difficult to allocate costs properly to each specific connection.

The traffic determines the variable portion of the cost of a connection. The pricing model adopted by the service provider can be applied to the same cost model with the same elements, even though some items may not have associated cost for some pricing methods. For example, a given telecommunications company (telco) may not charge for the ports and equipment, charging only for the last mile and varying the price with the bandwidth (PVCs). Another telco may charge for the last miles (the price varying with the bandwidth) and equipment (fixed price) while not charging anything for the PVCs. These examples show that different services and service providers allocate cost differently.

Using the model that associates costs with the technical entities allows for accurate determination of the cost, whatever it may be. Applying one consistent cost model for all pricing models helps to understand and consistently format the several pricing strategies. When elements are organized in the same way, costs can be compared fairly, leading to better decisions. See chapter five for a more detailed explanation.

In this book, we limited ourselves to aspects linked with techniques associated with traffic mapping and cost modeling. To be able to identify the ideal transport structure, we must be able to define our possible topological scenarios, map our traffic, and identify the transport cost available (own or subcontracted). We will be demonstrating:

- The techniques of topology identification (chapter fifteen)
- The techniques associated with data gathering and traffic mapping (chapter fourteen)
- Pricing models (chapters five and six)
- A brief discussion of outsourcing decisions (chapter seven)

Another aspect to be well understood is the difference between expenses and costs. The expenses associated with a telecommunications network often do not reflect the real cost of the structure.[4] In this book, when using the term *cost*, we assume all associated costs, including the depreciation.

---

4   This is given the fact that equipment is often bought and does not have a
     monthly cost associated or just has the maintenance cost associated.

5

Price Rules

Many different factors affect the cost of a WAN. From the obvious factors (geographic locations and traffic volume) to more subtle features (size of the service provider and ownership of network lines), an understanding of how one arrives at price and cost is required. When planning a WAN, it is crucial to have a complete view of the interconnection costs available.

This does not mean only knowing the typical costs in a given area, but also understanding to which factors the costs of the services are linked. It is very important to understand the rules applied when defining the transport prices. The manager must know how much it is going to cost to transport the required data and voice flows among the organization's sites.

5.1   Understanding Cost Drivers

There will be an interconnection cost. This is not dependent on building our own infrastructure or contracting it from somebody else. So we need to be able to identify this cost. This identification implies identifying the cost factors that the service providers use to define their prices.

We also need to identify the building costs. The identification of the interconnection's building cost is important even when the intent is to contract the interconnection from a service provider. It sets the minimum cost reference. For example, when asking for a quotation from a service provider for a 2Mbps link between two given addresses, where there is the possibility of installing a mini-link radio, it is advisable to know the cost of this radio if the organization installs it directly, even if the organization has no intention to do so. This knowledge makes it possible to compare this value with the service providers charges, thus identifying the services markups.

Identifying the parameters and factors that the service providers use to determine their prices is much more complex. It happens because, in most cases, we have some sort of artificial reasoning involved. Such artificialism usually comes from three reasons:

- Need for simplification
- Regulatory environments
- Crossed benefits (one service subsidizing another that is or is not motivated by regulation)

The interconnection costs can follow several types of rules, but the main factors defining the costs are usually:

- Bandwidth (nominal, CIR, or EIR)
- Distance
- Transported kilobits
- Spoken minutes
- Hourly distribution
- Area codes
- State border limitations
- National border limitations
- Inclusion (or not) of the CPE as part of the connection price
- Inclusion (or not) of management services

Telecommunications services are usually charged using three strategies: defined values per services, variable values (for example, charged on a per volume basis), or a mix of the two previous alternatives. Data access services usually have six cost components:

- The CIR, EIR, and nominal bandwidth usually define the costs of the PVCs.
- The maximum amount of ports and type of services supported usually define the price of equipment.
- Ports usually have their prices defined based on the speed (bandwidth).
- Last miles usually have their prices defined based on the nominal bandwidth.
- Management is usually a defined value for the network as a whole. This value is sometimes divided by the number of circuits and charged on a circuit basis.
- Taxes vary based on the country, state, and even city where the connection is installed.

These cost components sum to the total cost for data access service: PVC/connection/cloud(1) + equipment(2) + ports(3) + last miles(4) + management(5) + taxes(6) = Total cost.

Voice services usually have only three cost components defining the cost:

- Last mile is usually a monthly subscription fee.
- Usage is usually the value charged that is associated with a volume of spoken minutes. The values of the minutes may vary depending on the distance, hour of the day, area code, national/state borders, or day of the week. It is also common to find situations where a minimum amount of traffic is charged, regardless if it is actually used or not.
- Taxes normally vary depending from the country, state, or city where the connections are installed.

The formula for the total cost of voice services is therefore the sum of only three components: Last mile(1) + volume used(2) + taxes(3) = Total cost.

Although we may find variations of these basic components, in a vast majority of the cases, the prices will be defined based on this cost structure. How the tariff is structured is important to understanding and applying these simple-looking sums. Many times, the cost appropriation does not use all cost components. Often, this cost appropriation is divided between the two ends of the connection. For example, in a given phone call, the call originator usually pays for the subscription of his or her own trunk (last mile) and the traffic. The user receiving the call also pays for the subscription of his or her own trunk. In a situation like that, the match with the cost components described previously is as follows:

- **Equipment and port A:** Cost appropriation is zero, but this may not be true in some cases, such as when the telco provides the PBX (CENTREX services).
- **Last mile A:** This is the trunk subscription, which the call originator (caller) pays.
- **Cloud:** The cost appropriation is zero.
- **Last mile B:** This is the trunk subscription, which the receiver pays.
- **Equipment and port B**: The cost appropriation is zero, but this may not be true in some cases, such as when the telco provides the PBX.
- **Connection and traffic**: This tariff is usually charged based on the number of minutes (duration) of the call, distance, or hour of the day. The caller usually pays for the call.

In packet networks, there is *gateway sharing*. In this context, *gateway* is the name given to the last mile installed in the organization's main hubs in typical star networks to where and from where the connections flow. In these scenarios, the connections share the gateways. It is very important that the capacities of the last miles do not exceed the capacity of the gateways, even though some statistical maneuvers allowed that correlation to be different than 1:1. If they do, the flows will be limited to the capacity of the gateways. The nominal capacity of the last miles will be valid only until the border of the telco cloud. In this situation, the organization will be paying for bandwidth in the last miles that it is not going to be able to use. A practical tip would be to never allow the bandwidth in gateways to have a correlation with the summation of the bandwidth of the last miles below 1:0.6. In other words, the gateways should not have the capacity below 60 percent of the summation of the associated last miles.

Frequently, the service provider leads the users to believe that increasing the bandwidth of the last mile of one specific site is going to increase the available throughput. This is not always true. Gateway sharing limits this seemingly straightforward increase. It is important to be very aware of this likely source of wasted expense.

This situation is very common. An organization sometimes pays for the increase of the bandwidth (end A) without any significant improvement in the QoS. Very often, the gateway is oversubscribed, and the increase of the bandwidth in one end (A) merely increases the existing oversubscription rate. The organization pays more for no additional benefit.

To avoid this problem, the telecommunications manager should make sure that the summation of the CIRs contracted in the accesses cannot exceed the bandwidth available in the gateways beyond 40 percent unless it is an Internet access and part of the flow does not go to the gateways. It is just matter of keeping on doing the math. Keep your eye on the ball.

This sharing of the gateway, along with the fact that the cost appropriation is usually on an equipment and last-mile basis, makes it difficult to have a clear understanding of the cost associated with provide connectivity to each site. Using the model introduced in chapter four helps to clarify the specific parts of the cost breakdown. The costs are broken down as follows:

- **Equipment and port A:** Usually charged having the cost associated with the site A
- **Last mile A:** Usually charged having the cost associated with the site A
- **Cloud**: Usually has the cost appropriation equaling zero
- **Last mile B:** Usually charged having the cost associated with the site B
- **Equipment and port B:** Usually charged having the cost associated with the site B

- **Connection and traffic:** Usually charged having the cost associated with the bandwidth of the PVC defined to the site A

Because more than one connection (gateway sharing) uses the equipment and last mile B (gateway), it becomes difficult to accurately identify the total cost to provide connectivity to a specific site. It becomes necessary to proportionally divide the cost of the gateway among the sites using it.

Considering the importance of clearly identifying the cost to provide connectivity for each point of presence, when possible, the organization must require the service providers to present their prices end-to-end (connection basis). In a price format like that, all prices may be allocated to the end A. For the shared last miles (gateways), the cost would be zero.

The best way to avoid the common problems caused by gateway sharing and difficulty matching the pricing model to the cost factors just described is to contract the service in an entire connection basis (end-to-end). In this situation, the provider becomes responsible for guaranteeing throughput end-to-end, so it becomes its responsibility to adjust the gateways as connections are increased, reduced, or added.

The objective of a WAN is to provide throughput between two points. It is important to identify how much it costs to provide a given throughput between two specific sites. The cost to be analyzed is that of achieving the main objective of connectivity, which always requires complete connections (two points).

Although some cost structures consider connection cost end-to-end, the more common practice in data networks pricing is to only consider the access cost (last mile and equipment), charging the gateways separately as if they were a normal last mile. We are going to show some typical types of services and their charging structures. For example:

- **Leased lines:** The charging structure typically follows a function correlating distance and bandwidth. The cost usually covers both ends.

- **Optical fiber connection:** The cost is usually represented with a link between the distance and number of derivations (end-to-end).
- **Satellite connections:** The cost of this service usually correlates the volume in/out and antenna cost and a component associated with the hub cost (access and hub).
- **Dial-up access:** This normally follows a widely known price spreadsheet, which correlates destination (and distance), duration of the call, and, sometimes, the time of the day (or day of the week).

When collecting proposals, it is crucial to define the requirements accurately. It usually requires the preparation of a detailed request for proposal (RFP). The RFP will work to standardize the proposals. Without it, each provider will quote following its own standard and understanding, which would make the evaluation process very troublesome. When comparing proposals from different service providers, there are factors difficult to measure, such as level of control, quality of the technical assistance, and, of course, technological trends. In this book, when talking about proposals and evaluations, we are referring to economical aspects.

But even if we limit ourselves to the tangible factors (prices), it is very difficult to compare service provider's proposals. This difficulty exists for two main reasons:

- Reorganizing the WAN topology to take full advantage of the different interconnection alternatives is not trivial.
- The pricing strategies adopted by each service provider for different services may vary.
- Comparing proposals brings two sets of problems:
  - There is the issue of rearranging the network topology. To be able to identify the ideal WAN structure, we should be able to define all possible topological scenarios and verify the volume/flow for each topological scenario. Then we should be able to quote the interconnections with the service providers. By doing this, we will be able to take full

advantage of the different interconnection pricing strategies and prices associated with our specific geographical dispersion. However, identifying the possible topologies is not easy. Calculating the traffic volume/flows for each topological scenario is even more difficult. This problem is only solvable if we use design software.

- Even if we do not intend to rearrange the network topology, we can lock in the current topology to simplify the problem and ask the service providers to quote the interconnections for a specific traffic volume/profile. Even then, the comparison will be difficult due to the differences in pricing strategies adopted. Some services providers will charge based on bandwidth and distance. Others will charge on CIR. Others may charge a defined value for the cloud plus access.

Locking the topology[5] makes the calculations necessary to properly compare the proposals easier. However, very often, they are still not simple by any means. You have to know your traffic (volume/profile/interest) profile and be able to properly calculate all distances, CIRs, bandwidths, spoken minutes, and so forth in order to be able to calculate how much it would cost to transport each site's flow using each pricing strategy. You also need consistent breakdowns for each pricing strategy used by each service provider for each service/technology. Of course, everything is within a defined QoS. This is definitely not a trivial task.

Because of these difficulties, most organizations decide which services/technologies and service providers are going to be adopted based on intangible or tangible factors improperly calculated. Intangible factors include relationships with the service provider, technological trends, and individual preferences. The assumptions made in improper calculations normally include calculating based on monthly payment value only, assuming a defined topological scenario (usually star), and using only the current traffic volume.

This process has led to a situation where most WANs are far from ideally designed and usually have room for improvements. Carefully recalculating without these three limiting assumptions

5   Most telecommunications managers do exactly that in this situation.

(only explicit monthly payments, only one topological scenario, and only one traffic volume) can provide huge improvements. The key point to be able to take advantage of this potential for improvement is having the tools to do the necessary calculations. The use of interconnection cost calculators (programs to calculate the total costs of each connection) is important even if we did not analyze the topologies and routes. Consider the following example of price rules identification. For example, assume the following quotation for last miles based on bandwidth.

Banda total K	64K x	Custo last mile mês
2048	32	R$ 8.770,00
1024	16	R$ 5.350,00
512	8	R$ 2.830,00
256	4	R$ 1.559,99
128	2	R$ 1.000,00
64	1	R$ 650,00

The cost is associated only with the bandwidth. Based on the quotations and using nonlinear regression techniques, the function correlating bandwidth and price is determined to be as follows:

$$0.0001 * X^3 + 0.0434 * X^2 - 5.6862 * X + 414.63 = Y$$

X equals a 64K quanta, and Y equals price. This function generates the graphic below:

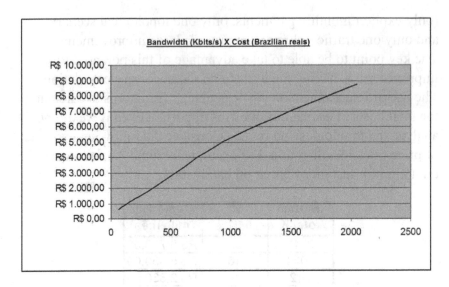

Understanding this correlation enables the manager to calculate the costs of any given bandwidth based on this specific pricing rule. It is the understanding of the rules that generated the prices that enables the manager to identify which proposal better suits the needs of the organization. One proposal may seem better at a first glance or with the current traffic volume, but, if there is an increase or decrease of traffic or if it changes the pattern, an apparently worse proposal may become the better one. This kind of planning may help the manager to define the better proposal by looking at not only the short-term but also the medium- and long-term time horizon. Decisions that are better for the organization over the life of the contract can be achieved with this understanding of cost drivers.

5.2   Comparing Proposals

To properly evaluate a WAN proposal, several steps are necessary. It is initially necessary to define a *standard scenario*. Such scenario in a voice structure would be the number of voice trunks in each site and a *standard bill* to which the prices in the proposals would be applied and whose total value would define the monthly cost of the proposal. We should also define an *expanded scenario*. Such a scenario in a voice network would be an expanded number of trunks in each site and an *expanded standard bill* where the initial volumes are increased by a given percentage, which is usually the expectation of organic growth during the lifespan of the contract. The same logic applies to a data network or an integrated voice and data structure.

The total monthly expenditures can virtually always be calculated as the sum of each type of element. That is, the volume of the components of traffic multiplied by its associated per-unit transfer cost. These elements are then added to get total cost. For example, the number of minutes times the per-minute charge plus the number of links times the per-link charge and so on. The determination of the total proposal cost has several steps:

- Calculate the basic and expanded monthly values.
- Calculate the TCO of the whole structure during the contract lifespan. Besides the direct monthly cost paid to the telco, that also requires considering the following factors: installation costs, migration costs, expansion, and internal cost to manage the solution.

Once the basic monthly cost has been determined, calculate these additional items to have a complete understanding of the proposals. These costs are then applied as though monthly (costs amortized over the life of the contract). The basic idea is to bring all costs to a monthly basis, allowing for a proper comparison.

5.2.1   Calculating the Monthly Value of the Installation and Migration

To normalize the installation and migration costs to a monthly basis, the perpetuity financial calculation is applied using the following parameters: contract duration (N months) and monthly interests t percent a.m. (based on WACC of the organization).

We should assume a uniform series of payments for a defined period of time (contract duration). This mathematical technique allows for identification of how much the initial payments[6] would represent on a monthly basis. Seeing all proposals on a monthly

---

6   Installation is usually charged up-front.

basis is crucial to being able to compare them. The behavior of the calculation is demonstrated below in picture 10:

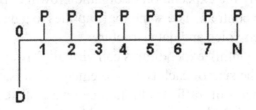

Observe that the installation and migration costs made in the beginning of the contract D would be paid along *N* months. To find the value of the monthly parcel (*P*), use the correlation between the parcel (*P*) and the total value (*VP*), as demonstrated by the formula below where:

$$VP = P \times \left(\frac{(1 + i)^t - 1}{i (1 + i)^t} \right)$$

- VP = Installation/migration value (detailed in the proposals)
- i = Interest (X percent a.m.) (based on WACC of the organization)
- t = N° of periods (duration of the contracts)
- P = Value of the parcel (to be identified)

Using the formula, identify the installation and migration value on a monthly basis. The value linked with the advantage of the current provider is based on the cost of migration and values associated with paying penalties. There are expenses that would not exist if the incumbent provider were kept. These are added to the proposals of other providers and not to the incumbent's proposal. Installation cost is diluted into the monthly parcels. This expense is also likely to favor the incumbent. These two values, once identified, sum to the basic monthly value of the proposal. This, along with expansion costs and internal costs associated with the proposal, allows accurate comparison and ranking of the proposals.

5.2.2 Expansion Costs

Ranking the service providers' proposals based exclusively on the current volumes is not enough. It is also necessary to calculate the costs of an expanded scenario. This expanded scenario is necessary for good planning because traffic volumes can be expected to increase. Traffic volume has increased drastically over the past decade, and it will likely continue to do so with ever-increasing database sizes even if an organization does not grow in number of users or locations. Considering the need for new circuits or bandwidth at the time of the initial contract may save money. New circuits may cost more as they are added near to the end of the contract. Increasing gateway bandwidth may be extremely expensive.

To be able to do these calculations, it is necessary to know in advance the value to be charged for additional resources during the contract lifespan. This is why such values must be quoted and used to calculate the costs in an *expanded scenario* during a quote evaluation.

The calculation of the cost of an expanded scenario will indicate how much the network would cost if the traffic volume increased by x percent. This calculation is attainable executing the design again but using the future volume. With this analysis completed, the manager will have the ranking properly calculated, reflecting the best alternative over the life of the contract.

5.2.3 Internal Cost Associated with the Proposals

Evaluating the scenarios present and expanded may not tell the whole story, even though this is better than most organizations, which do not even do the expanded scenario calculations. To identify the precise ranking of the proposals, the internal cost to manage the contracts must also be calculated. A proposal may seem cheaper in the present and expanded scenarios, but it demands more internal management effort. For example, if a proposal does not specify that the bills are going to be provided in digital media, this is going to demand a resource be contracted to consolidate these bills. This additional cost must be added to the cost of the proposal. This is the concept of associated internal costs.

A calculation of this cost, combined with the costs calculated in the previous items, it is what really gives the organization the right perspective about the economical merits of each proposal.

6

Negotiating with the Service Providers

Negotiations with service providers are part of the function of
a telecommunications department in a large organization. In
these day-to-day negotiations quotations, proposals, and requests
are made regularly, and technical and economical aspects are
discussed. Negotiation skills are therefore assumed to be one of the
basic skills of the typical telecommunications manager in a large
organization. But even with experienced negotiators, negotiating
large corporate WANs is always a challenge.

The negotiation of a large corporate WAN involves strategic
aspects not present in the day-to-day negotiations. The financial
numbers are high, the transition processes are lengthy, several
aspects such as QoS are not easily mapped, and service providers
are usually large corporations with experienced negotiators. All
these reasons make proper planning essential.

In a typical organization, a complete renegotiation of the
contracts supporting the WAN usually takes place at intervals not
smaller than three years. Often, intervals even longer than three
years elapse between contract reviews due to the rooted habit
of just renewing existing contracts. This law of least effort of
choosing to stay in the same contract even when it may not be the
best choice is one thing to overcome when negotiating. Regular
negotiations are necessary to achieve the best results.

Considering the complexities involved, it is advisable that
the IT or telecommunications manager faced with the need to
renegotiate the organization's WAN must initiate the process at

least one year before the actual renewal date. This is typically the time required to make a proper assessment of the current situation in terms of traffic per service, defining the strategy, identifying appropriate designs, and preparing a detailed RFP.

6.1 Considerations Prior to Negotiations

When negotiating a WAN structure, try to make all services contracts terminate at the same time, and, if possible, standardize the contract's lifespan. This will enable maximization of mix and size of services to be quoted/contracted. Frequently, it is not possible. However, this situation usually can be achieved within one or two cycles of the typical contract's lifespan. This standardization can also be achieved by extending existing contracts or making all new site services part of a existing bigger contract with a single coterminus end date.

Frequently, competitive local exchange carriers (CLECs) and incumbent local exchange carriers (ILECs) in different countries own the entire range of services, from mobile telephony to providing leased line services utilizing their own infrastructure.

When the providers can offer an entire range of services, the telecommunications manager may manage to aggregate services increasing the overall size of the financial pot they are competing for. This strategy often makes possible the achievement of better prices.

6.2 Negotiation Strategy

Planning the negotiation strategy is key to successful negotiations. The process must consider several key factors that the makeup and culture of the organization typically determine. As an example, the telecommunications manager must evaluate the organization's disposition to manage and trust its providers. These are typically some of the factors to be evaluated regarding the organization itself and its needs, the environments where the organization operates, and the providers available when planning a WAN negotiation process:

- Agility required from the provider companies[7]
- Organizational capabilities of the organization in different countries or regions of the globe
- Degree of centralization or decentralization of the IT infrastructure and decision-making
- Degree of telecommunications deregulation in countries of operation around the globe
- Language barriers
- Degree of local knowledge of telecommunications industry in other areas of the globe
- Ability or desire to manage multiple vendors and finance systems with different currencies, languages, cultures, and accounts payable environments
- Differences of control and capabilities in regions of the world over different technologies like voice, mobile voice, and data networking, which are often the result of an organization's historical growth and acquisition strategy
- Management's view of outsourcing

Control issues are another political issue that organizations find easier to ignore than to question. Questioning and analyzing the existing control structures will either validate or clearly show that a strategy is not adequate to maximize use and efficiencies of technology tools. Sometimes, even the best technology is not suitable for a specific dysfunctional control structure. The people defining the negotiating strategy have to complete such analysis. A strategy is clearly required when entering into service provider negotiations. The strategy should address the following points:

- Clear statement of global approach to service providers, for example:
  - One global provider (or one provider by country or region)
  - Providers with local capabilities and infrastructure in areas of operation
  - Best use of local providers in their areas of operation

7   Telecommunications companies are very process-oriented, which results in organizations that are not very dynamic in their mode of operation.

- Local or a universal language capability in regions of the globe
- Finance capabilities, currency requirements, and payment terms
- Provisioning and sales cycle time frames

- Aggregation of all communication spending up for renewal by category with line items broken out for each of the following:
  - Outsource options
  - Voice mobile, private, fixed and public switched telephone network (PSTN)-based services
  - Conferencing services, including Web, voice, and video
  - Video streaming services
  - Remote access services
  - Data connectivity
  - High availability

- Clear internal understanding and communication regarding network capacity and QoS requirements
- Positioning the ideal topology based on flow analysis and geographical realities driven by political, organizational, and other regional influences
- Positioning at least two transport strategies[8]
- Defining specific contractual elements up front, including:
  - Cancellation and penalty clauses
  - Accounts payable and dispute arrangements

- SLA components
  - Penalties and contract cancellation conditions
  - Technology refresh options
  - Help desk performance metrics

- CPE ownership and management, which regional regulations might dictate
- Standard price lists[9]

---

8   This might have to be regionally based.
9   This is often desirable in decentralized organizations, and it has many advantages in the areas of cost appropriation and financial planning. This price

Considering the complexities involved with some of the topics listed, it is advisable to start planning at least one year before the actual renegotiation. Of course, the time frame depends on the size and complexity of the network. It is our experience that the people executing this kind of work frequently display a lack of preparedness when negotiating a WAN. It is also very common to find people negotiating these structures whose view is purely economical. This view usually generates two very typical approaches:

- **Kick-the-telco approach:** There is no complication. We quote with all providers and just choose the cheapest one or force the one we want to get to the price we want.
- **Minimalist approach:** There is no need for detailed specification. Just send the providers the list of things we have today.

These views, although not entirely wrong and may work for a small infrastructure, do not consider a fundamental factor of this process. When negotiating a complete WAN, we are not only comparing the prices per service, but also comparing the prices of the different transport strategies. An example of comparison between different transport strategies is as follows, and it is the main problem with the kick-the-telco approach:

- **Comparing the prices against the cost of a private voice network:** The cost of the spoken minute has to be compared not only against the others service providers' prices but also with the cost to transport them through the private voice network.
- **Mobile traffic:** The cost of the spoken minute fixed-mobile cannot be compared only with the fixed trunks providers, but also with the alternative of providing dedicated mobile trunks installed in the PBXs to transport fixed-mobile traffic.

---

averaging is often only possible in regional settings. Even though it might provide a simplified operational structure, it is inevitable that some operational entities will pay a price penalty. That said, the advantages to central planning, financial visibility, and overall simplicity in a large, multinational network is significant.

In addition to the above, the services contracted today may not reflect the actual organization's needs, which may have changed since the last negotiation assessment. This is the main problem with the minimalist approach. Therefore, when preparing to renegotiate the WAN, it is crucial is to accurately map the traffic, understanding perfectly from where to where it flows, the volume, quality requirements, and available transport strategies. In other words, before discussing technologies or contacting the potential providers, the telecommunications manager has to understand very well the organization's current and future needs in terms of traffic volume, interests, and profile

The fact we are not just comparing the costs per service but also the costs per transport strategy is a fundamental point and does make a difference when negotiating with telcos. Besides the possibility of comparing different transport strategies, the only other alternative is the direct comparison between the same services. In this situation, each telco usually knows the limits of the others. The chances for driving down costs are limited. (This is usually associated with the volumes.) There is very little room for discounts. In this situation, there is a big chance that the current provider, who already has its investment paid for, offers the best price.

Large organizations may have several telecommunications providers. They usually concentrate their business with a few of them. Typically, between one and three providers are responsible for 80 percent of all telecommunications expenditures. This strategy has the advantage of simplifying the operation and enhancing the relationship with the chosen providers.

However, we should be aware to avoid exaggerating this concentration of business. It may trigger overconfidence by the providers and loss of contact with other alternatives available in the market. We often hear comments like, "We don't want to have several providers." There is a fine line here, and no one should see having few providers as an end in itself. It is only worth as long it guarantees better prices, simplicity, and leverage.

In addition, when contracting services, it is always convenient to allow all providers to offer their services, even when they are not able to cover all network POPs. The basic logic must be, "Provider, quote your best price where you have coverage." Never put having few providers as a prerequisite when doing a quotation. This is an easy path for higher prices.

Adopt the logic of allowing all potential providers to present their best prices where they have coverage. There is no obligation to quote services for all POPs . This implies that you are not ruling out the possibility of having several providers. But it does not necessarily mean contracting in this way.

Eventually, a quotation can be done, allowing the providers to offer services only where they have coverage. Later, you may narrow down the options to the ones with wider coverage, using the cheapest prices of all proposals as negotiating references.

Although common, contracting only one service provider may not be advisable. Having at least two main providers may be better due to commercial and technical reasons. Commercial reasons are based on competition and the reduction in cost of moving services between existing suppliers, as opposed to bringing in a completely new service provider. From a relationship point of view, it is always good to create a situation where a service provider knows there is a concurrent competing contract to whom the organization can easily turn for its requirements. Technical reasons are based on security and risk mitigation. For example, it is advisable to use backup circuits contracted from a different provider than the one providing the primary circuits.

Of course, contracting a complete WAN, including the CPEs, with more than one provider may have its difficulties. A provider may have technical and/or commercial restrictions in allowing other providers to connect resources to its devices. This problem is rare though. In most cases, the quotations are done assuming that each provider will have its own CPEs, although this will vary between regions of the globe.

The management of multiple contracts may be seen as problematic, but, considering the fact that a typical telecommunications area already manages several contracts, although concentrating services into a few of them, this argument seems to lack substance. If the internal people are not able to absorb this small amount of additional effort, something may be wrong with the way the organization manages its telecommunications contracts.

Segmentation may reduce volumes. Telecommunications managers may see this as tending to reduce the discounts offered. This argument, however, has several problems:

- This strategy does not eliminate the possibility of a provider offering all services in all areas (if it is capable to do so).
- This argument does not consider the already mentioned fact that we have to compare not only service providers and services, but also transport strategies. (One transport strategy may be applicable only in some areas.)
- Maybe more problematic, we may have potential providers whose prices are very good but limited to some specific geographical area. Depending on the percentage of our services within these areas, even if we pay a lot more for the services outside those areas, the savings could still be substantial. (See chapter thirteen for examples.)

With all these ideas in mind, we have to structure the quotation process. The quotation should be structured in such a way that the service provider must present a defined price per connection, and these prices must be associated with defined parameters. It enables visibility and transparency when contracting new services or changing/canceling existing ones during the contract life cycle, which will surely occur.

6.3 Pitfalls to Avoid

When preparing a RFP or a request for information (RFI), it is very important to avoid some basic pitfalls. We are going to list some of the more common ones:

- **Price visibility:** Very often, service providers are reluctant to present defined price lists, using the argument that, if they

present a defined price list, they will be punishing the client
once the prices go down because they will not be able to offer
those prices. They will have to follow the price list. We don't
buy these arguments. The difficulties associated with visibility
of the telecommunications costs of new sites, including
the possibility of the prices going up instead down and the
difficulties linked with quickly verifying costs associated with
a specific provider, surpass many times the benefits of the
service provider's hypothetical decreased future prices.

- **Gateway cost:** A marketing practice prepares quotations of
  packet networks based only on the equipment and last miles
  costs. Such a quotation strategy generates a situation where
  the gateway cost has to be paid separately. This charging
  strategy makes it difficult to clearly identify the connection
  cost per site and very often generates problems of over/
  under capacity for such gateways. The ideal is to avoid it
  when possible. However, we know it is not a decision that is
  entirely in the telecommunications manager's hands. If all
  potential providers refuse to charge in a per connection basis,
  the telecommunications manager may not have a choice. We
  recommend to try to do in this way always. It does not mean
  you are going to succeed in 100 percent of the cases. Knowing
  the ideal does not mean you always will be able to do it.

- **Backup structure:** When contracting backup circuits, the
  fact that it is not ideal to contract the main and backup circuits
  from the same provider should be given serious consideration.
  A single provider, even if the provider has two different
  physical infrastructures, will still expose the organization to
  administrative problems, which may affect the provider, such
  as strikes, bankruptcy, and so forth.

7

Practical Tips for Outsourcing Networks

When dealing with the subject of outsourcing WANs, *outsourcing* means contracting hardware and services outside the organization. It is important to understand a basic concept. Unless the organization owns all transmission means and all equipment and manages its own NOC to some extent, it will be outsourcing part of its network to a service provider. Therefore, in the absolute majority of the cases, WANs are outsourced, even if only partially.

In the telecommunications context, the term *outsourcing* applies only when the equipment and the management is contracted with the service provider. People do not usually say the network is outsourced when only the means (circuits) belong to a provider and the equipment belongs to the company. From our perspective, this is a mistaken view. All of them are outsourcing processes with the only difference being the degree.

It is very rare to find situations where the organization owns all WAN components and operates them itself. This kind of situation happens more often in organizations such as petroleum companies, railways, highway operators, and governments. These organizations usually build their own networks. Building its own network is more typical for service providers. Even then, they may subcontract parts of their infrastructure.

In a more common situation, where the organization does not own its whole network, we have WANs outsourced in many different levels. It may have its transmission means contracted from a telco, which is not usually perceived as outsourcing, or its equipment rented with maintenance contracted from a telco or hardware vendor. The organization may have its NOC services contracted with a telco or service provider. It can finally have its own telecommunications personnel contracted through a personnel outsourcer.

In most cases, we see a combination of these outsourcing scenarios. Although outsourcing has been in and out of fashion several times and sometimes was even sold as a panacea, the experience led us to have a more cautious approach to the pros and cons of this process.

It is important to clarify that there is no point in being for or against outsourcing. As mentioned, practically all organizations, to some extent, outsource their WANs. In the end, the issue is to evaluate how each outsourcing strategy is to be implemented and to be able to see the advantages and disadvantages of each particular strategy as it applies to your organization's requirements and culture.

The outsourcing of the means is practically the rule among organizations. Normally, only the companies that own tracks of means interconnecting their sites will build their own infrastructure, for example, petroleum and gas companies, railways, and highways operators.

Other exceptions where outsourcing is not considered a valid alternative use are government organizations whose considerations are not purely economical, such as to prevent reliance exclusively on public networks. This includes armies, security agencies, and natural disaster agencies.

Giving an additional emphasis to the analogy with the transportation system, we would have a situation where a company could contract the truck or railway's companies directly or contract a company like UPS or FedEx to manage its storehouses and transport your goods. In the same way it happens between ILECs/CLECs and carriers, a company like FedEx may subcontract a truck company, which, in turn, would use a public highway. Outsourcing the equipment is also very common, but the way it is done encompasses some variations. For example:

- Rent the equipment and contract the maintenance and management from a hardware vendor
- Contract the equipment and management from a telco
- Rent the equipment and maintenance from a hardware vendor and the management from a service provider
- Buy the equipment and contract the maintenance from a hardware vendor and the management from a service provider
- Buy the equipment, contract the maintenance from a hardware vendor, and perform the management internally.

Other combinations are possible, but these are the more common ones. At this point, we have to understand the conflicts of interest that make some of these combinations not so suitable.

Initially, it is important to understand that the equipment (WANs switches, routers, or PBXs) are essentially resources that enable the management of the telecommunication means. This management, in theory, is executed through selecting lowest cost routes and managing the traffic flows. Because of that, there tends to be a conflict of interest between who provides the means (circuits) and who provides the equipment. We are going to illustrate this situation with the examples below:

- **CENTREX service (PBX provided by the telco):** What interest would telco one (owner of the PBX) have to configure the PBX to redirect calls to telco two when the call through telco two has a lower cost? Assume optimistically that telco one would allow the trunks belonging to telco two to be installed in its PBX.
- **Bandwidth optimization resources:** What interest and/ or diligence would a telco have to implement bandwidth optimization resources in its equipment if, when doing so, these resources will reduce the need for bandwidth and reduce the values paid by the client?

These examples highlight the issue of contracting equipment and means from the same telco. When an organization adopts this strategy, it is quite likely that the telco who owns the equipment will deny access to other service providers to them. Even if it does allow other providers to install their trunks, it will resist requests to configure it to redirect traffic to other provider trunks (CENTREX service example). The telecommunications manager may try to force them to play nicely together,[10] or it may buy or rent its own equipment and link all providers to them. The equipment may or may not belong to the company and may or may not be managed directly by it. Some intermediary alternatives can be negotiated as well, such as you can see the configuration but not change it, or you can see and change, but not beyond this point.

The outsourcing of the network management is even more delicate in terms of conflict of interest. If the hardware provider is responsible for the hardware maintenance and network management, it will tend to be condescending with equipment problems (its own faults). In this scenario, the hardware provider will have a vested interest in disputes with the telcos and tend to attribute the problems to them, avoiding the fact that the problems were related to the equipment under its own responsibility. On the other hand, if the entity responsible for the management is the same entity responsible for the telecommunications means, the same problem described previously will occur, but with the issues reversed. We often hear the magical solution: Let's put the means, equipment, and management under the responsibility of the same entity. This is the worst-case scenario. Once we put the responsibility for identifying problems entirely in the hands of the service provider, it creates a situation where a service provider punishes itself financially when it identifies its own faults. This is definitely not a really effective strategy for the organization. Surprisingly, this is a very common situation, and it tends to generate a high level of stress between the provider and the organization.

From our perspective, the ideal scenario is when the organization outsources parts of the structure to different providers with one or more entities responsible for the means or circuits, one responsible for the equipment maintenance, and another for the network management.

---

10   Very large organizations may be able to do that.

A rarer situation is when the telecommunications department is itself outsourced. In this scenario, the internal personnel are contracted through another company. In this kind of situation, we must be extremely cautious regarding conflicts of interests. The ideal is never to contract the internal people from a company who provides any other service (network management, maintenance, or means).

Related to personnel outsourcing, there is an increasing trend to outsource telecommunications and IT help desk environments. Some of these responsibilities are outsourced to countries with low labor cost. This is only effective when the outsourced help desk is carefully managed and given the tools and documentation to execute effectively on its mandate. The cost-benefit analysis of such outsourcing must include the cost of providing this support.

The economical argument for outsourcing makes sense theoretically. An organization that provides a large number of telecommunications resources tends to have a smaller cost per served unit than one with a smaller volume. There are two problems with this argument:

- Very often, the companies that present themselves as outsourcers are not the owners of the network. They subcontract the infrastructure from one or more telcos. Although it is true that these companies tend to get smaller prices from the telcos due to the volume, it does not necessarily result in better prices for the final clients. Very often, the operational cost of the outsourcer accounts for the difference between the value that the client would pay if contracting directly from a telco and the cheaper price that the telco originally gave to the outsourcer. This problem becomes more acute as the size of the organization grows because the difference between what the organization can obtain negotiating directly with a telco and the value obtained by the outsourcer narrows significantly.
- If the outsourcer is a telco and actually owns the infrastructure, it will tend to treat the process as if it were a conventional proposal (selling circuits/means), just adding additional

services to manage the network by an in-house team. This tends to eliminate scale gains and add services to the telco bill.

A company trying to decide between purchasing equipment instead of relying on a service provider must consider a combination of factors. The obvious comparison is between up-front capital and ongoing maintenance costs associated with purchasing equipment versus leasing similar functions from a service provider. Additionally, there are more intangible issues related to things like control, for example, level of responsiveness, bundling, and leverage. Does the person who needs to fix the problem actually work for me, or am I dealing with a contractor over whom I have less leverage? Generally, three interrelated factors qualify the feasibility of outsourcing a telecommunications structure:

- **Size of the company:** Generally speaking, for large corporations, it usually makes sense to buy equipment and hire staff to maintain it.
- **Rate of growth:** If a company is growing quickly, there is a danger of outgrowing the infrastructure before it is time to replace it.
- **Expertise of staff:** In terms of staff, some companies have a large telecommunications/IT department and like to do things in-house. Others prefer to stick to their core business and leave the care and feeding of their telecommunications networks to others.

There are some gray areas when deciding whether to outsource a telecommunication network or not. But we should keep in mind that the main motive for outsourcing is usually savings. However, when evaluating the achievable savings, we should consider not only how much the organization is spending today but how much it could be expending if doing everything in-house in the best way possible.

Most outsource evaluations are based on the actual company's expenditures compared with the foreseen outsourced price. The problem with this practice is the fact that, in most cases, the company could be doing a much better job in-house than it is actually doing, so the comparison between actual expenditures and outsourcing is not fair or in the company's best interest.

Therefore, in order to rationalize the decision of whether to outsource a network or not, it is absolutely crucial to identify the optimized in-house cost and then use this value to evaluate outsource alternatives. Using the actual cost as reference can give you the wrong perspective about the benefits of the strategy.

Some may argue that savings would be achieved anyway, no matter if you use the current value as reference or identify the possible minimal in-house cost. We particularly believe that having a correct base of reference for cost is crucial in this process. Only when the theoretical ideal cost is known can the real benefits of outsourcing be defined.

Very commonly, the potential outsourcers do the homework of analyzing the WAN, identifying the potential gains, and defining the price based on the current cost. In this situation, the outsourcer will take advantage of the organization's lack of knowledge of its own needs and possibilities.

In summary, the decision to outsource encompasses many considerations. Knowing what is already outsourced, being aware of potential conflicts of interest, and having a thorough understanding of economic considerations are all-important. It is only possible to fairly evaluate the cost benefits of various outsourced solutions when you have an accurate view of the costs to build and properly manage an in-house optimized infrastructure.

8

The Impact of New Applications on the Network

Discussions about software quality improvement mostly center on things such as bugs and security vulnerabilities. Unfortunately, little of that software quality rhetoric has focused on issues related to network performance and cost. Applications affect network performance. The effects on performance and cost deserve more attention from IT managers ahead of deployment time than they often receive.

This oversight is surprising and not at the same time. It is surprising because we have been wrestling with networked applications for well over a decade now and we know all too well how representative the network cost is in the overall IT budget and how poor performance impacts our operations. On the other hand, it is not very surprising because application development teams and network technicians are known for not interacting as much as they could. Application developers are taught to focus on business use models, code quality, and project management disciplines. Efficient use of network resources remains a relatively low priority in most of the IT world, especially with network technologies evolving to make more and more bandwidth available for the asking.

In general, the network team accepts the application's demand for bandwidth as a consummate fact without questioning it. The predominant mentality is "We start from there" or "Our job is to transport whatever the applications demand." The usual situation is such that no one in the network team has or wants to have any say during the application development process.

There is a different approach. Thorough evaluation regarding the impact of the traffic generated by each application over the network (LAN/WAN) should be done for any new application deployment. This should be done even in the early stages of an application's development. The impact in terms of network cost/ performance should be a major factor in defining the feasibility or not of implementing a new application or its chosen architecture. Considering the percentage of the typical IT budget that the telecommunications/network represents, it would be reasonable to expect these analyses to be standard procedure.

Instead, we usually see that applications may be tested in advance for stability, user acceptance, and CPU utilization, but their behavior on the network remains an afterthought. No one really knows:

- How they will perform across the diverse LAN and WAN connections they must traverse
- How they will impact the numerous other applications traversing those same connections
- How efficient in terms of bandwidth utilization they really are (or could be)
- How much they will add in the cost of the network until they go live

Analysis of network impact is needed not only when implementing brand-new applications, but also for other changes. Sometimes adding a new feature to an existing application can wreak havoc on the network. Other times, it is the addition of a new site or new users. Developers often fail to fully comprehend the impact that adding Web-based access to a legacy application can have on both hosted Internet infrastructure and enterprise connectivity.

This situation cannot be attributed exclusively to the lack of interaction between application development and network operations, although it is an important part of the problem.

The difficulties associated with modeling the impact of a new application over a preexisting network go beyond lack of inter-team communication. Even when having a well-oiled, experienced team, it is difficult to put together all pieces involved in order to properly model the problem. Most people may imagine that it is only a matter of properly measuring the traffic that the new application generated and extrapolating this traffic throughout the whole structure. Unfortunately, reality is a bit more complex.

Even if the new application traffic is measurable and the new application usage patterns can be reasonably identified, we still would have to have a clear view of the whole current structure, including things such as:

- Current traffic (other applications)
- POPs
- Interconnection possibilities (including service providers and technologies)
- Possible aggregation scenarios to be able to properly identify the more cost-effective way to handle the new traffic

A new application with a new traffic volume/pattern may make it economically feasible to deploy different technologies, service providers, or even a different topology.

Experience shows that, the sooner the telecommunications team participates in the process of developing software, the smaller the chances of experiencing problems with the implementation of a system. Additionally, it will result in minimizing the financial impact associated with the telecommunications costs.

To avoid this problem, it is important to include the telecommunications/network team in the process of creating new applications. The sooner the better. Every new application must be developed considering the impact it is going to have on the company infrastructure, not only on the telecommunications network, but also servers, storage, and so forth.

9

Managing the Telecommunications Area in an Organization

The organizational structure and area of responsibility of telecommunications within large organizations have been changing over time as shifts in technology took place. Generally, the objective of this rearrangement has been to bring telecommunications into the IT sphere of influence, unifying voice and data disciplines in the telecommunications/network area.

The migration of the telecommunications area from "general services" to "information technologies" is an administrative trend, which follows the technological trend of integrating voice and data over the same network.

The proper management of a telecommunications area demands a serious organizational effort. The telecommunications/ IT manager must identify not only the tasks involved, but also the necessary skills requirement of the professionals who execute these tasks and the workload involved. Such task mapping allows the precise definition of the necessary workforce if the whole operation was in-house or reference values for outsourcing.

The organization must clearly define the tasks and responsibilities of the telecommunications area and identify the ones that it intends to execute in-house and the ones that will be outsourced. The job descriptions of the staff members must indicate the tasks and responsibilities of each professional and the workload involved. This enables the identification of under/ overallocation of personnel as well as the identification of technical deficiencies (if any) solved through training and redeployment of people.

The goal is to provide the organization with all the necessary instruments required to effectively manage the telecommunications infrastructure. Such instruments include an appropriately sized, trained, and organized team where each one knows his or her responsibilities and is well prepared to execute them, clearly defined processes and policies, and complete infrastructure documentation.

The objective of this chapter is to provide a general view of how to organize a telecommunications group within a large organization. The following organizational aspects need to be considered: processes (operational and technical, cost control, documentation and administrative, and planning for expansion); operational and technical policies; norms and procedures; and data management.

9.1 *Processes*

The processes required to manage the telecommunications infrastructure must be carefully planned. But planning is not enough. The processes need to be executed correctly and consistently. It is not important if it is executed by the telecommunications area, some other functional group within the organization, or outsourced company. The four main types of processes are:

- **Operational and technical:** Keeping the structure running
- **Cost control:** Keeping track of how much the organization expends with telecommunications
- **Documentation and administrative:** Keeping track of the resources and its configurations
- **Planning for expansion:** Preparing for new services and matching demand with availability

These four main groups of processes may be subdivided as follows:

- Operational and technical
  - Help desk operations
  - Voice trunks and data links monitoring
  - PBX management
  - Voice mail management
  - Incoming call control
  - Routers management
  - WAN switches management
  - Network security management
  - Cable plant management
  - Technical management of telecommunications contracts

- Cost control
  - Telephone billing control
  - Billing system management
  - Telecommunications costs internal appropriation
  - Outgoing calls control
  - Expenses approval

- Documentation and administrative
  - Telephone list preparation and distribution
  - Equipment and resources physical location control
  - Network diagrams
  - Administrative services

- Planning for expansion
  - Capacity planning
  - Evaluating new technologies

The division of processes is arbitrary. Our only aim is to simplify the explanation. Also note that all processes have linkages with each other. The objective here is not to describe the processes themselves, but just to list them and give the reader a brief view of which tasks it encompasses. We are going to briefly discuss each one of them.

9.1.1 Operational and Technical

Operational activities are the ones directly linked with keeping the telecommunications infrastructure running. These are the technical tasks involving configuring equipment, monitoring the resources, and interacting with the users and service providers. We grouped these activities into nine macro-processes, although some of them are interrelated. As already mentioned, this division is arbitrary and aims only to simplify the explanation.

9.1.1.1   Help Desk Operations

All tasks involved with attending to users' requests and registering these requests are help desk processes. The execution of this process requires some level of technical knowledge and the possibility of consulting the organization's knowledge base to identify known issues. Of course, this demands the preexistence of some sort of software where the requests, issues, and problems are documented. Ideally, the organization already has an IT help desk to which the requests regarding telecommunications can be forwarded. If there is not a structured IT help desk, it will be necessary to organize a specific telecommunications help desk, even if it has only limited resources. If the organization does not have some sort of organized process through which telecommunications problems are registered, the people of the telecommunications area will tend to spend a high percentage of their time attending to requests directly from the users instead of solving those problems. This becomes more critical as the size of the organization grows.

Help desk operations may be outsourced (chapter seven), but the processes and documentation described here still apply. In fact, the process documentation becomes even more important when the people executing the tasks are not local and not in-house.

A clear escalation procedure needs to be in place and communicated to the organization to catch any situation that may result in a customer satisfaction issue. Often, all the business needs is the assurance from senior management that the appropriate resources are deployed to address an issue.

9.1.1.2   Voice Trunks and Data Links Monitoring

Activities linked to the managing and monitoring of telecommunications resources include, but are not limited to, monitoring the trunks and links, identifying problems, and monitoring utilization rates to identify under/overcapacities. This activity is very important as the level of utilization of the links and trunks is key in guaranteeing the necessary level of service. Through this task, the organization also manages and determines the demand per service. For example, mobile traffic or long-distance and international traffic can be separately monitored. Ideally, issues and problems can be identified before they impact the user.

9.1.1.3   PBX Management

This process encompasses all tasks linked to managing and configuring of the organization's PBXs. It includes the configuration of least-cost routes, extensions, trunks, and users. It also includes the maintenance of the PBX's databases.

Although parts of this process are usually relegated to the PBX providers and included as part of the PBX maintenance contract, it is the responsibility of the telecommunications area to ensure the entity responsible for PBX configuration has the correct information to ensure proper PBX configuration. It is also the responsibility of the telecommunications group to verify that the configuration was properly implemented, for example, least-cost routes and criteria of trunk group selection.

Quite commonly, people in charge of managing the telecommunications area do not understand or know how their PBXs are configured. This is a significant issue. A PBX configured inappropriately may result in substantial additional telecommunications costs.

The ideal situation is to have a carefully prepared PBX configuration plan in order to standardize the PBX operations throughout the organization, indicating the specific configuration to be implemented in each machine. Special attention needs to be paid to maintaining and keeping the configuration backups updated. It is not uncommon to experience problems related to reloading configurations from backup after a hardware failure because those configurations do not reflect reality. In this scenario, every user whose extension was installed or changed since the last backup gets his or her telephone wrongly configured. So it is crucial to have backup of every change in the configuration.

9.1.1.4 Voice Mail Management

This process includes all tasks associated with managing the organization's voice mails. These activities include updating the voice-mail software database and monitoring the voice mailboxes. Unified messaging extends this function to include interfacing with an organization's e-mail systems.

9.1.1.5 Incoming Call Control

This process includes all tasks linked with the control of the incoming calls. Incoming call control is only possible in the sites equipped with BINA devices (B identifies A). The billing system usually registers the incoming calls. The professional in charge of these tasks will use a specific application to consolidate the incoming calls and select the ones of special interest. This task is particularly important considering security aspects, for example, hoaxes, threats, and so forth.

9.1.1.6 Router Management

This process consists of all tasks likened with managing and configuring the routers. It includes tasks such as route configuration, IP numbering, cryptography applications, QoS, and user access control. The control and maintenance of all aspects linked with the routers and related databases are grouped into this category.

This configuration function needs effective monitoring and control by the telecommunications area. Failover policies, the least-cost routes, and combination of flows over physical routes are aspects closely connected to the telecommunications contracts and WAN design. This is an important aspect of the telecommunications department's mandate.

Although it is common to find the responsibility for managing the routers outside the telecommunications area, the ideal scenario is running this function in-house for the reasons mentioned before.

9.1.1.7 WAN Switches Management

This process includes all tasks linked with managing and configuring the WAN switches. This task includes routes configuration, PVC numbering, failover strategy, QoS, and user control. The control and maintenance of all aspects linked with the WAN switches, related databases, and configuration all fall under this type of process. Today, there is a general trend to merge the functionalities of the so-called WAN switches with the routers.

Very often, such equipment is under the service provider responsibility. In this situation, the telecommunications people tend to treat this equipment as part of the connectivity service. Such approach, although common, is not ideal. We may have scenarios where more than one service provider connects its last miles into equipment managed by one specific service provider. This situation, although rare because most service providers just do not allow last miles from other providers, forces the telecommunications team to be extra careful with the configuration used on the equipment. It is very important to be able to see the configuration and define how the traffic is divided between the last miles of the several providers, preventing the owner of the equipment to take advantage of the situation against the best interests of the organization. This kind of problem also happens when we are trying to use compression devices and sophisticated flow control devices.

9.1.1.8 Network and Network Security Management

Network security is a primary concern of modern IT/ telecommunications departments. Although these fall outside the main area of responsibility of most telecommunications mangers in large organizations, it is important to know what security is used on the network, including software applications for security purposes. These all affect network traffic. Processes include selecting and implementing proxies, DNS management, firewalls and intrusion detection devices, and antivirus software. Also, procedures for response to security breaches or other events fall under this category.

9.1.1.9　Cable Plant Management

This process involves all aspects of managing and documenting the cabling infrastructure in the organization's premises. This includes documenting the infrastructure, problem solving, managing subcontractors, and managing moves and changes.

The telecommunications area is responsible for keeping track of (controlling and documenting) all wire distributors (voice and data) and the cabling of the organization's premises. It is crucial that each cable in each patch panel be properly identified and documented. Frequently, the telecommunications area does not maintain the cabling plant directly, but it needs to enforce documentation standards verifying if everything was properly installed and identified. This is equally true if the responsibility for the cabling has been contracted to a service provider. The data requirements must be spelled out in the contract if the process is outsourced. In all cases, it is very important to have a defined process and procedure describing how to install and how to document moves and changes.

The importance of accurate documentation cannot be overemphasized. It is the basis of what enables a telecommunications area to provide remote (level two) support. This is particularly true in large organizations where the people providing support have no way to know how the cabling is installed at each site unless it follows a predefined standard.

9.1.1.10　Technical Management of Telecommunications Contracts

Telecommunications contracts need to be managed and their QoS and SLA levels verified. This type of activity demands time and effort. It is a mistake to assume that the existence of control tools and rigid QoS clauses in the contracts by themselves guarantee that failures will be identified and penalties applied. The processes must be not only documented, but also executed and audited to ensure effective execution.

It is interesting to note how often we see extremely rigid QoS clauses in contracts without a correspondent process in place to verify and punish the deviations. This situation makes a highly debated SLA (with additional associated costs) useless in the day-to-day running of the contract. So it is advisable that all SLAs be easily verifiable through proper tools and the process, from the problem identification to the application of penalties, be clearly defined and all stakeholders have their responsibilities very well defined.

A failure to actively manage the SLA components of contracts leads to a situation where SLAs are merely guidelines of operation when the relationship between a telecommunications provider and the organization has deteriorated to a point where constructive interaction is not possible. When the impact of failure is significant, this needs to be reflected in the SLA agreement and possibly the failover design of connections.

9.1.2 Cost Control

All activities linked with controlling the costs of the telecommunications infrastructure and the activities linked to internally appropriating this cost fall under the cost control processes. It is important to emphasize the need for having a well-defined process to receive bills, match them with the actual usage and the resources actually in use, approve the payments, and properly register and distribute these costs internally.

9.1.2.1 Telephone Billing Control

This process encompasses all tasks related to receiving bills from the telcos (in electronic media or in paper) and matching them with the resources actually contracted and the real usage. The organization should be able to process these bills in order to identify the expenditures by address, business unit, provider, and type.

The auditing of the bills can be subcontracted to an external provider and executed on a regular monthly basis, or these audits may be executed on a quarterly or semestrial basis. Although the auditing itself may not be executed monthly, the values verification and comparison between the values charged with the historical values needs to be done every month in a continuous way.

It is crucial to establish a process where every telecommunications invoice must be verified by the telecommunications area before it is paid. This applies to all telecommunications charges within the organization. Approval by the telecommunications area before payment prevents potential contract issues or missed steps in the process. The telecommunications area must be responsible for verifying both that the bill is part of a valid contract and the value charged is actually due. Only then the bill should be forwarded back to the accounts receivable department.

An effort should be made to consolidate the bills, that is, avoiding each site receiving its own bill. This consolidation should happen in an electronic media. No telecommunications invoice, including telephone bills, should be paid directly by the users. The telecommunications area must also be responsible for conducting the discussions about undue charges, penalties, and reimbursements.

Time limitations should also be included in contracts to limit disputes to a reasonable time frame of six months to a year, including verbiage related to service availability during dispute periods.

9.1.2.2   Billing System Management

This process involves all tasks linked with managing, maintaining, and controlling the billing systems. It is very important to properly evaluate the correlation between the cost of having a billing system and the savings achieved through it, mostly in the small sites with low traffic volume.

It is crucial to maintain properly configured billing software and updated databases. Accurate information must reflect any changes in users, extensions, cost centers, organization's hierarchy, tariffs, and least-cost routes. These support tasks make the billing process effective.

To maintain accurate data, it is very important to establish processes that will keep the telecommunications area informed of new as well as departing users to the organization to facilitate timely action, for example, blocking the extensions, mobile phones, and so forth. These processes are frequently localized HR processes, but a failure to link them to telecommunications departments may have cost as well as security implications.

9.1.2.3 Telecommunications Costs Internal Appropriation

This process encompasses the tasks linked to telecommunications cost appropriation to the several business units and cost centers of the organization.

In a telecommunications network, shared resources can make the proper cost appropriation far from simple. First, we have to clearly understand the concept of shared resources. The following example describes shared resources and some of the difficulties of appropriation of their costs. As described previously, a connection may share ports, equipment, and last miles. A clear understanding of this concept is important because it is going to have important impact regarding cost appropriation and the management of the resources. The following picture gives us a clear view of what physically happens.

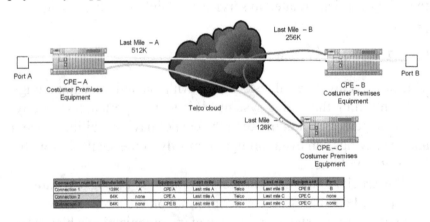

Connection number	Bandwidth	Port	Equipment	Last mile	Cloud	Last mile	Equipment	Port
Connection 1	128K	A	CPE A	Last mile A	Telco	Last mile B	CPE B	B
Connection 2	64K	none	CPE A	Last mile A	Telco	Last mile C	CPE C	none
Connection 3	64K	none	CPE B	Last mile B	Telco	Last mile C	CPE C	none

As we can see in the picture, the equipment and last mile A are shared for the connections 1 and 2, dark grey and light grey, respectively. This fact implies that the costs of these resources must be shared on a connection-by-connection basis, the cost to provide connectivity to each point of presence.

It is important to clearly define the sharing criteria before proceeding with a cost-appropriation strategy. (See the Expenses Approval section.) For example, divide the resource monthly cost in the same proportion of the bandwidth used. In the case of last mile A specifically, we have two connections, one of 64K and another of 128K. Using the criteria mentioned before, we would have a cost appropriation as follows:

- Y = Last mile A monthly cost
- Value appropriated to the connection 1 for the use of the last mile A = $128 \times Y/(128 + 64)$
- Value appropriated to the connection 2 for the use of the last mile A = $64 \times Y/(128 + 64)$
- 64 and 128 are the bandwidths of the connections 1 and 2 respectively, both using the last mile A.
- The cost of the connection will be the sum of all entities associated with the connection (seven items).

This cost appropriation may also be mired in political issues within large diversified organizations when business units are themselves large organizations and choose to pick from central services those services that they perceive to have a direct benefit to them. This may lead to different agendas on the part of business units that detracts from aggregating costs to the advantage of the overall organization. This area needs careful consideration. Keeping the billing and cost appropriation as simple as possible should be a primary goal of the telecommunications.

9.1.2.4   Outgoing Calls Control

This process is closely related to the billing system management, but includes task such as consolidation and analysis of all calls originated from the sites and eventual chargeback to the users for private calls.

This process has to be carefully implemented. Otherwise, the control may cost more than the value saved. A good access-restriction policy may be more effective than trying to charge the users retroactively for unauthorized calls. The ideal situation is to combine an adequate access restriction policy, for example, limit the access to international and long distance to special extensions, with verification by exception, for example, verify only the international and long-distance calls whose duration exceeds two minutes.

Another interesting type of solution is the use of prepaid extensions or users, where each extension or user receives a predefined volume of minutes per month. Above this value, there is the need for new authorization of minutes.

The adoption of billing systems and access restriction policies tend to reduce the telephone costs between 10 and 20 percent (between 20 and 30 in the first month). So it is undoubtedly an important resource. Other aspects to be understood is the fact that, through the billing systems, it becomes possible not only to control the usage for cost reduction proposes, but also to manage needs such as requirements for mobile phone trunks.

9.1.2.5 Expenses Approval

It is important to have a clear process where every telecommunications expense, besides the recurrent bills, can only be paid after the telecommunications area has approved them. Very often, organizations do not adopt this policy. It is very common to have the business units paying bills directly and only communicating the costs to the telecommunications area afterwards, but this is sometimes not done either.

It is also advisable to give some level of autonomy to the telecommunications manager to approve small and recurrent expenses. Such autonomy should be enough to allow small maintenance expenses. Of course, the term *small* varies, depending on the organization's size.

This task of expense approval, billing, and cost appropriation has different levels of complexity, depending on an organization's profile in terms of geographic spread of business units. Telco costs structures vary significantly between different regions of the world.

For companies with a large international footprint, the picture becomes very complicated.

For example, a single, low-cost America- and Canada-wide wireline long-distance rate may be easy to negotiate in North America. The mobile phone costs in Canada are typically significantly different from those in the United States and will usually incur a different long-distance rate from mobile providers. If such an organization has a presence in Mexico, it complicates matters considerably due to the significantly different charging regime. Now spread this organization over thirty countries, each with a different voice-charging structure and a view of how and where the money is spent. This becomes very important to the point that it should drive network design decisions.

There has been a growing regulatory and organizational trend to emphasize financial transparency. Financial transparency has become an absolute must for senior management. This area is frequently woefully inadequate in large, decentralized organizations. Expense approval plays a pivotal role in financial transparency. When done correctly and following clear processes every time, expense approvals support very clear financial documentation and transparency. When not done appropriately, this leads to inaccurate budgeting, cost control, and, ultimately, a telecommunications environment that is not (or cannot be shown to be) running as an effective entity.

9.1.3 Documentation and Administrative

Documentation and administrative processes record the details of the infrastructure, including inventories of business units, users, extensions, addresses, POPs, equipment, last miles, connections, contracts, configurations, and administrative services associated with these processes.

9.1.3.1 Telephone List Preparation and Distribution

This process includes all tasks linked with preparing, maintaining, and distributing the organization's internal telephone directory. Although the physical directory printing and folding may not be typically executed by the telecommunications area, its preparation has to be. Today, most companies do not even have a printed directory anymore that relays exclusively in online-only directories. It is necessary in order to keep the directory in line with the moves and changes implemented in the PBXs and contracts.

It is quite usual to have a situation where each department updates its own data in a common directory software. This strategy, although practical, tends to generate directories with a high level of mistakes and not in line with what was actually implemented by the telecommunications area in the PBX configuration.

In order to avoid such problems, operational uniformity must be guaranteed (administrative versus technical). It is crucial to have the telecommunications area in charge of controlling the organization's internal telephone directory. It is the only area that can ensure data integrity. The telecommunications area must have the responsibility to guarantee the uniformity of the information in the PBXs, voice mails, billing systems, and internal telephone directory.

This directory maintenance function will vary depending on the maturity of overall directory services in an organization and its PBX technology deployment. An organization with a mature identity management environment will typically have the phone directory integrated as a component of its overall directory and identity management implementation. In this case, the maintenance of the directory will be with a different IT department. The telecommunications area will be responsible for its interface into the bigger directory environment, and the validity of the information

9.1.3.2 Equipment and Resources Physical Location Control

In large organizations, it is very common that the telecommunications resources inventory is not well controlled. As time goes by, equipment and resources are relocated, deactivated, or returned to service providers without proper documentation. This leads to a very common situation where the telecommunications management does not have an updated inventory of the resources under its responsibility.

To guarantee this inventory is updated, it is necessary that all people involved in reallocation of resources follow defined processes documenting any canceling, changing, or moving. The telecommunications area must control these procedures directly. This includes tasks such as physically controlling the equipment (own, rented, or subcontracted), including routers, PBXs, WANs switches, racks, cable modems, and so forth.

It is crucial that the information repositories be properly maintained and a system be in place that controls this as master data. It should be possible for the organization to query all aspects related to any service, equipment, or contract.

9.1.3.3   Network Diagrams

This process includes all tasks linked with preparing and maintaining the network diagrams. It is crucial to have proper network diagrams depicting the network as a whole (see below) and diagrams showing the configuration of every site and rack. The general diagram must show all organization's POPs, all WAN devices, all last miles, and connections. Such diagrams must allow the identification of every device under the responsibility of the telecommunications area and must be used as a day-by-day tool by the telecommunications team.

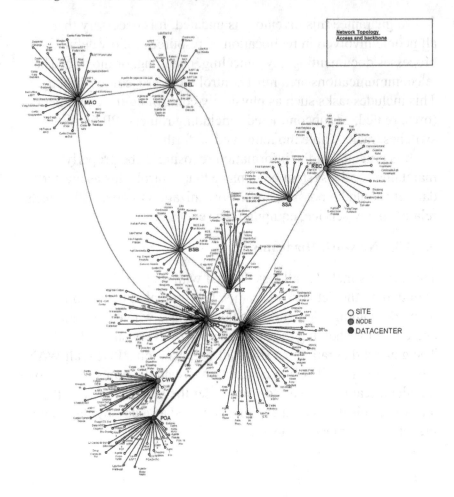

9.1.3.4   Administrative Services

A telecommunications area needs administrative support, including document forwarding, data entry, and so forth. There may be no need to have dedicated administrative personnel because the IT administrative pool may be enough, but, depending on the functions executed by the telecommunications area, we may have a need for dedicated administrative personnel.

9.1.4   Planning for Expansion

We must have a very clear process defining the planning of the network that should include defined processes to include the telecommunications area in the discussions about new applications and defined processes to identify changes in the demand and how to address those changes.

9.1.4.1 Capacity Planning

The telecommunications area should be attentive to the changes in the demand, trying to anticipate those changes. Through the monitoring tools, the telecommunications area should be able to analyze if the resources available are adequate. Over/under capacity situations need to be identified before affecting user services in an adverse manner.

It should also participate in the discussions about new services and applications, indicating to the organization the impact in terms of telecommunications resources (technical and economical) of including or removing services. It is also crucial to have processes in place that gives the telecommunications area some sort of insight about site expansions and organic growth. It should be done within a defined process, not sporadically. This process needs to involve the top level of management in both the IT and telecommunications area on at least an annual basis to demonstrate due diligence in the overall planning process.

Physical expansion of the network is often an interesting situation as it is common for organizations to expand by acquisition. These are generally not announced even internally to an organization until a deal is done. In these cases, the telecommunications area needs to be part of the IT due diligence function as a large acquisition could have a significant impact on both usage and cost base of the telecommunications infrastructure.

9.1.4.2 Evaluating New Technologies

This is not a daily process, but there can be a consistent approach to evaluating new technologies. The group of activities that are part of this evaluation must be documented and consistently executed to keep current in the technological world. It is a matter of due diligence of the telecommunications area to scan the market, looking for products and solutions that may add value to the business of the organization. It is advisable that the technical people have access to magazines and conventions where they can compare their own experience with other professionals. It is very important that the organization provide resources for this function. Otherwise, this will increase the influence of service providers and hardware vendors to a point that is not in the organization's interest.

All functional resources should keep abreast of current technology. Some companies have a structure that includes functional resources like network architects. These individuals may have the primary responsibility for their own technical areas. However, the entire team should know what technologies are available and how they can apply to the organization.

The telecommunications area is also responsible for training the users of the telecommunications resources, letting them know how to take the most of the available resources.

9.2   Operational and Technical Policies

The proper definition of operational policies is a prerequisite to the effective operation of a telecommunications infrastructure. The telecommunications manager must know the types of policies that are in use or needed in the area. These policies then need to be clearly defined. The definition of these policies implies predefined operational strategies that invariably touch the telecommunications area, demanding a very clear understanding of the overall organization's IT strategy. It is not our intention to make recommendations of specific policies because those are very dependent on the organization's specific needs. We are only listing some of the typical decision points:

- Contracting strategy for equipment and means (same providers for equipment and means or not)
- NOC operation (in-house or outsourced)
- Resources acquisition (rent, buy, or lease/periodical hardware renew)
- Support and maintenance strategy (permanent technical assistance contracts or as-needed requests)

- Strategy to receive the users' requests via a help desk
- Expenses-approval policy
- Technological standards
- Level of participation of the telecommunications area in the organization's IT decision process
- Definition of the telecommunications resources demand standards
- Definition of the policy of resources control and documentation
- Definition of the policy of IT/telecommunications costs appropriation
- Training policies
- Global infrastructure standards
- Regional policy decision points
- Global policies affecting regulatory requirements
- Global change control policy (usually part of an overall IT change control policy)

All the above listed definitions must be discussed internally. Once defined, they should be properly followed. The organization must avoid that such definitions occur by default following the circumstance or convenience of the moment. Ideally, these definitions should reflect a corporate posture and must be completely compliant with the overall IT policies and strategies. Of course, these policies should not be static. They should follow the changes in the organization's needs.

It is our experience that policies and standards should be defined globally as far as possible. This enables an environment where teamwork and cross-regional support becomes possible, greatly enhancing the efficiency of the human capital deployed across the organization.

Here we emphasize the need for having unified inventory databases, processes, and technological standards. Sometimes, the several arms of a large organization spread around the world do not understand the benefits of unified policies (standards) well. Each telecommunications team in each country tends to believe that its own ways are the best, but anyone who had the chance to manage a large multinational telecommunications area will know that having a standard is better, even if you are not going to be optimal in every environment.

9.3   Norms and Procedures

For a telecommunications area to operate properly, it needs adequate operational procedures and guidelines. This section lists typical guidelines and procedures. It is not our intention to define the norms themselves. Those depend on the context of each organization. This list will provide a reference point and explain the aim of each type of procedure. The telecommunications managers must detail them for their specific environments. In these guidelines, we indicate the responsibilities, frequency of the procedures, and, above all, who can do what and when, for example, who can request a specific report and how this request should be done. The following twenty-one general topics cover the main areas of responsibility of the telecommunications manager. Note that these cover all areas of IT and telecommunications, from operational to cost control to capacity planning. This list expands upon network maintenance and security operational tasks mentioned earlier in this chapter. The main procedures needed in each area are listed:

Help Desk Operations	Structured processes with clear procedures are needed for the following: Request for information regarding problems with the telecommunications infrastructure (placing a help desk call)
	• Registration of the request through the IT help desk
	• Generation of an internal services ticket
	• Definition of criteria to attend or not to a request
	• Analysis about the treatment to be given to a request (solution

	internal or external) • Control of activities of internal personnel, different levels of control, or provisioning services • Evaluation of the need for buying miscellaneous materials or services • Request services from service providers • Request services of internal personnel • Control of the recovery time (real) and matching it with the contract and calculating the penalties (if any) • Closing the maintenance tickets
Voice Trunks and Data Links Monitoring	Processes must be defined for the following: • Defining the criteria for decision-making regarding problems in equipment, links, and trunks and when and who to escalate • Management of the bandwidth and trunks availability (capacity planning) • Alerting mechanism for fault and capacity management problems
PBX Management	Procedures must be defined for the following management tasks: • Definition of criteria to access the PBXs • PBX databases maintenance • Configuration changes • Backup procedures

Voice Mail Management	Norms must define the access to the voice mails, including procedures and operational rules: • Criteria for using the voice mail • Procedures to enroll, change, or cancel a user in the voice mail system • Criteria to define maintenance of the voice mails to avoid undue disk space usage
Incoming Call Control	Procedures must define how the incoming calls will be controlled: • How the business units select and inform the incoming telephone numbers to be verified • Configuration of the devices to filter the desired incoming calls • How the reports are generated and distributed
Fax Management	Norms defining how the fax servers are going to be managed, including procedures: • Database maintenance, server configurations, and operation (password, numbering, space allocation, and operational logs) • Reports generation
Router Management	Procedures and guidelines defining the router management: • Database maintenance, router configurations, and operation (password, numbering, tables allocation, and operational logs, version control)

	<ul><li>Reports</li><li>Alarm monitoring with level of importance, including the procedures associated with each alarm</li><li>Failure identification and understanding</li><li>Security mechanism and strategy</li><li>Traffic measurement and network performance (buffers, CPU load, memory available, protocols, and interfaces used)</li><li>Graphical view (physical) of the network devices, allowing the display of ports and equipment status visualization</li><li>Automatic equipment discovery, map creation, and status updating</li><li>Information regarding users and maintenance of a device</li><li>Mechanism of software management and distribution</li><li>Documentation, including design and strategy information detailing route policy decisions and so forth</li><li>QoS policy implementation</li></ul>
WAN Switches Management	Procedures and guidelines defining the WAN switch management:<ul><li>Database maintenance, WAN switches configurations, and operation (password, numbering, tables allocation and operational logs, and version control)</li></ul>

	• Reports • Alarm monitoring with level of importance, including the procedures associated with each alarm • Failure identification and understanding • Security mechanism and strategy • Traffic measurement and network performance (buffers, CPU load, memory available, protocols, and interfaces used) • Graphical view (physical) of the network devices, allowing the display of ports and equipment status visualization • Automatic equipment discovery, map creation, and status updating • Information regarding users and maintenance of each device • Mechanism of software management and distribution • QoS policy implementation
Network Management	Norms defining the proxy/DNS management and the associated procedures: • Database maintenance, equipment configuration, and operation of the proxy/DNS servers • Alarms monitoring and types of problem classification • Internal and external DNS procedures and its integration with Active Directory

	• Problem identification • Security mechanisms • Graphical view (physical) of the devices, allowing the display of ports and equipment status visualization • Access to equipment statistics • Global DNS load balancers (GLSBs) and their policy implementation, also including failover policies implementation in the event of catastrophic failures in a shared global data center
Network Security Management of Firewalls	Procedures defining the management and configuration of firewalls/intrusion detection devices: • Level of information integrity • Information responsibility • Confidentiality • Responsibility of the telecommunications area as it relates to security devices
Network Security Management of Antivirus and Security Software	Procedures defining the management and configuration of antivirus/Trojan/spyware software and prevention of denial of services and other attacks and the associated procedures: • Management, configuration, and mechanisms of protection and removal • Configuration, patches updates, and parameter definition • The role of routers and WAN

	switches in containment procedures when experiencing a security event • The role of telecommunications staff in the containment procedures when experiencing a security event
Cable Plant Management	Procedures defining the physical control of the cabling plant: • Standard definition of icons, flows, colors forms, documentation, and drawing applications • Drawings preparation • Controls process and procedures
Technical Management of Telecommunications Contracts	Norms and procedures defining the technical management of contracts: • Tracking of contracts of equipment, including its costs and feasibility of replacement • Tracking of services contracts • Maintaining a database with contract details that enables queries to be run against various aspects that make up a contract • Early notification and renegotiation of contracts about to expire
Telephone Billing Control	Norms regulating the telecommunications expenses management: • Process of receiving and treating the bills • Process to receive and register telecommunications expenses

	<ul><li>Process defining internal appropriation of telecommunications expenses</li><li>Process for monitoring and controlling outgoing call expenses</li></ul>
Billing System Management	Guidelines and procedures defining the management of the billing systems:<ul><li>Data collection</li><li>Databases maintenance (workers, passwords, extensions, tariffs, and telephone usually accessed)</li><li>Management reports</li><li>Maintenance regarding changes to master data</li></ul>
Expenses Approval	Procedure that defines the expenses approval function:<ul><li>Approvals (who signs documents) for level of values (level of competence)</li><li>Who checks expenses against contract specifications for accurate billing</li><li>What tools and mechanisms are used for validation of the various services</li><li>Definition of contacts and dispute agreements and mechanisms per provider</li><li>Procedure for feedback into the approval validation from the monitoring function to ensure that contracted SLAs were delivered</li></ul>

Documentation Controls	Procedures defining how the documentation control is going to be executed: • Standards definitions, icons, flows, colors forms, documentation, and drawing applications • Drawings preparation • Links to other procedures; for example, change control needing a check for the requirement to update documentation
Telephone List Preparation and Distribution	Procedures defining how the management and publication of the internal telephone list is going to be executed: • Define frequency of publication and media for online access to the phone list • Define integration with global directory services or identity management systems, monitoring and controlling of data transfer between telephony and other directory services.
Administrative Services	Procedures and guidelines defining how the administrative services are going to be organized: • Mailing, letters, memos, and faxes • Contracts terminations and changes • Invoice verification, expense control, and process of expense approval • Costs appropriation (internal) • Expense control and report generation

Equipment and Resources Physical Location Control	Procedures defining the process of physical control and transfer of equipment: • Equipment moves and changes • Physical relocation • Activation and deactivation of equipment • Change control procedures and verification controls • Disposal of used, redundant equipment • Physical access to equipment • Environmental control, which may be part of a general IT environmental monitoring and control procedure
Evaluating New Technologies	Norms and procedures defining the evaluation process of new technologies and personnel training: • Definition of various levels of interest • Procedure for matching organizational requirements to technology solutions • Process defining evaluation criteria, cost definition, and vendor relationships • Business case justification procedure and guidelines • Establishment of periodical meetings with users to evaluate the performance of the resources in use • Training plans and attendance of staff at technical conventions as appropriate

The telecommunications manager should review each of the listed tasks to ensure that procedures are in place for those that apply to the organization. Especially in smaller organizations, many items listed above may be included in one procedure. Procedures ensure consistent execution of all processes within the functional areas. They also facilitate training of new personnel and qualification for quality standards, such as ISO certification.

9.4 Data Management

The telecommunications area must control information related to the infrastructure. These data elements are described below. However, our objective here is not to exhaust all the possible elements that could exist but only give the reader a general view.

- Internal telephone list: Business unit, hierarchy level, people, trunks, and extensions.
- Equipment: Detailed list of all equipment under its control, including owned, rented, leased, and telco-owned equipment.[11]
- Last miles (including voice trunks): Database of last miles including location, capacity, costs, technology, CIR, EIR, nominal, equipment linked to, telco ID, and service provider.
- Extensions: List of all extensions cross-referencing the PBX configurations with the internal telephone directory.
- Contracts: Database including resources contracted, service providers, price list, termination conditions, init and finish, and recurrent cost.
- People: Database including all people who use the infrastructure and people who may or may not be employees.[12]
- Providers: Database indicating all basic data regarding each provider, including address, person of contact, function, telephone number, e-mail, support procedures, and provider escalation procedures.

---

11 The list must include all detailed data regarding the equipment, such as type, model, manufacturer, serial number, capacity installed and available, software version, maintenance contracts, and so forth.

12 This database must be associated with the PBX configurations (users and passwords) and with the internal telephone directory and router managers (including router passwords and management tools users).

- Topology drawings and internal cabling documentation.
- Moves, changes, and problems tickets (including ones covered by contracts and those that are not).
- Change control documentation, approval, and validation controls: Normally aligned with the rest of the IT department.
- Invoice control (expenses): Database indicating the costs per business units, cost centers, last miles, address, provider, and contracts.
- Equipment configurations: Routers, WAN switches and PBX .

Accurate maintenance of these databases not only serves the organization, but the IT/telecommunications department itself. The telecommunications area is the primary user of most of this data. Regular maintenance done by consistent procedures will make many of the tasks of the department easier and more effective.

10

Implementation of a New WAN Infrastructure

In this chapter, we provide a general view of how a process of migrating/implementing a new WAN should be structured. The section describes some of the general principles that must be considered in the implementation of a new WAN infrastructure. The intent is not to describe general project management, but it assumes that established project management disciplines will be applied to the project.

Implementing a new WAN design or migrating to different service providers is a complex process and needs careful planning and management. The planning function should clearly define risks. The aim should be no disruption to user services during the migration period. All players on the implementation teams need to understand the impact of disruptions.

In terms of human effort, the implementation of a WAN is a high-demand process. The major impact on the human resource requirements of the telecommunications area is often not clearly understood and sometimes massively underestimated. Adequate planning on this level is frequently not done, leading to problems with the project or in the ongoing production operations during the implementation period.

The implementation of a WAN involves several groups working together and whose effort has to be articulated. The work of the team planning the implementation is to guarantee that all participants work in a coordinated way and receive all necessary resources (information and materials) timely.

The participants involved can be divided into three basic groups: the team responsible for coordinating the implementation, the new providers, and the former providers.

The new providers are responsible for telecommunications means and hardware for the new WAN. The former providers are responsible for the current structure (if any). Except for some rare exceptions when the former provider maintains part of the services, the former providers are in process of terminating their contracts. This is usually with a high level of reciprocal dissatisfaction, and they do not have any particular interest in the transition process. The clear understanding of this reality is very important for the team planning the migration. Each structural group (the internal team, the new providers, and the former providers) can be divided into three others based on function:

- Telecommunications means providers
  - Main network data circuits providers
  - Backup network data circuits providers
  - Voice trunks providers
  - Mobile services providers

- Hardware providers
  - Large PBX (or voice switches) providers
  - Small PBX (or voice switches) providers
  - Router and WAN switches providers
  - NOC equipment and software providers
  - Miscellaneous equipment providers
  - Network management services providers

- Teams responsible for the physical infrastructure
- Internal teams
- Subcontracted teams

Each one of these groups can include several work teams and can belong to a several organizations, and there may be overlap.

It is not our objective to detail the necessary documentation, but just explain how the process must be structured in general and list the items that must be considered. The implementation planning of a new WAN structure includes the development of detailed documentation. The objective is to provide every team with all specific information and a general view of the whole structure, allowing the understanding of how each part fits in the whole. This understanding is crucial because it guarantees that all involved have the right perception of the importance and implications linked with the part under its responsibility. The migration process usually demands the preparation of the following documents:

- Migration plan
- Subcontractor's working plan
- Data network configuration document
- Voice network configuration document
- Inventory of all resources contracted from telcos
- Infrastructure inventory and documentation (including cabling diagrams)
- Contingency plans during the installation
- Definition of how the site will operate

The team in charge of planning and coordinating the implementation must prepare these documents in advance. They must be read and discussed with the teams of the providers. We are going to discuss each one of these documents.

10.1 Migration Plan

The migration plan is a group of documents giving a general view about how the new network is going to be physically installed and configured and how the transition is going to be done. Some of these documents provide the technical overview and design documentation. This document is usually written with the following structure:

- Documentation general view
- Telecommunications structure general description with all general information (LAN/WAN)

- General description of the voice network
- General description of the data network
- General description of the installation strategy
- Administrative information and list of the network elements
- PBX configuration spreadsheets (small and large)
- Router configuration spreadsheets (small and large)
- WAN switches configuration spreadsheets
- Operation configurations
- Components description of each site
- Project chronogram

10.2 Subcontractors Working Plan

This is typically the task breakdown, linkage between tasks, and timeline definitions. It would typically have milestones and detail dependencies between different teams. The work plan documentation also details the configuration of the equipment to be installed by each team (hardware installation teams) and physical diagrams of each site (for the infrastructure teams). These documents include both technical aspects (details of the procedures and configurations) and aspects like the responsibilities of each team and timelines foreseen (dates and deadlines).

In addition to the information related to tasks and actual implementation elements, this documentation must also include the databases related to the configurations themselves (for example, users, extensions, trunks of the PBXs, and so forth) and the administrative information related to the process (for example, site complete address; site responsible including e-mail, mobile, and pager; and site special instructions).

The project manager needs to ensure the various installation teams clearly understand these plans. At this point, it is important to keep in mind that hardware vendors frequently have default configuration implementations. If the organization does not define how the equipment is going to be configured, the hardware vendor will not always do it in the optimal way for the organization. They will configure the equipment in the simplest way that demands the least effort possible. They usually adopt the default configuration, which just guarantees the basic functionalities of the equipment and does not guarantee that functionalities, such as least-cost routes or fail action sequences, will work properly. If the configurations are not properly defined, documented, and explained to the installers, they will tend to follow the least-effort law and use the default configuration.

The team coordinating the installation must remember that there is a conflict of interest between the installation teams and the organization. From the perspective of the installation team, the quicker and with least amount of effort the equipment is installed and handed off to the organization, the better. This does not consider the validity of the configurations. It is the responsibility of the organization's team to check and verify that the configurations were properly implemented.

So it is crucial to have a clear definition of the configurations and how they are going to be verified. Without that, there is a significant risk of configurations issues due to errors or omissions that may be identified only when the network does not react as planned in the event of a failure or through high operational costs, for example, if the least-cost routes are not properly implemented.

Improper or a poorly setup network results in problems that frequently follow the network through its lifetime. When detected, long after the installation, it incurs significant costs to correct.

10.3 Data Network Configuration Documentation

The data network documentation must include the detailing of the following items. Such items must make it possible for the technicians involved to understand how the structure should work, even if they are unfamiliar with the organization's environment. Reading this documentation, the technicians must be able to configure properly all resources. This documentation should include the following:

- General description
- Diagrams
- Topology general view
- General view of the network elements

- General view of the nodes interconnections
- Configuration premises
- Description of the TCP/IP structure
- LAN network
- General view of the WAN routing
- Special connections (per segment)
- PVC/DLCI identification
- Router backup dial sequence
- Voice devices configurations (PBXs)
- View of the equipment installed
- Contingence plan
- Test sequence

The test plan needs to incorporate all the elements that will properly verify the configurations. Equally important is the fact that, even if the configuration adopted is the default, that must be clearly indicated in the documentation. Security needs special mention here as it is not uncommon to have easily identified user IDs and password settings. A good practice is to use a defined set of passwords and then have the internal team change those to internal security standards after verification of configurations and handoff from installation teams.

10.4 Documentation and Configuration of the Voice Network

In the same way described in the previous section for the data network, the telecommunications implementation team must prepare a detailed description of how the voice network is to be installed and configured. It is very common to find organizations where the responsibility for the PBXs configuration is entirely left to the hardware provider's discretion. This situation, although common, is completely unacceptable. It is absolutely crucial that the organization's internal implementation team plan the equipment configuration and verify that it is implemented properly. Aspects such as least-cost routes, redirection for specific services, and standardization of procedures are factors that generate large savings and productivity gains, although demanding some additional configuration effort. Leaving the definition of such requirements to the hardware vendors has the following problems:

- The hardware vendors do not know the organization's contracts and tariffs and have no way to know how to configure the equipment properly.
- The hardware vendors do not know the organization's operational standards. In a heterogeneous environment, the internal team is responsible for defining the standards throughout the organization, regardless of brands and models.
- The hardware vendors do not have a particular interest in expending additional effort to implement specific configurations, even if these configurations generate savings to the organization. So, if we leave the definition of the configuration to the hardware vendors, there is the tendency to make this configuration as close to the default as possible.

With these facts in mind, the team coordinating the implementation must prepare detailed documentation defining exactly how equipment must work and provide all necessary specific details. A documentation of a voice network should include the following:

- General description
- Small PBXs
    - External outgoing calls routing configuration
    - Internal outgoing calls routing configuration
- Large PBXs
- Diagrams
    - Topology general view
    - General view of the network elements
- General view of the voice network
- General view of the connections between WAN switches (PBXs and routers)
- Exchange lines
- Security
- Dial plan

- Features access codes
  - Feature-related system parameters
  - Class of services (COS/COR)/access codes/system parameters
  - Extension categorization
  - Users categorization
  - Class of service permissions
  - Class of restriction permissions
- Least-costs routing
- Extension numbering plan/patching schedule
- Telephone keys configuration/digital phone layouts
- Telephone models
- Key systems/Hunt groups/cover patch
- Direct-dial-to-extension flow in the nodes without send calls active
- System abbreviated dialing
- Voice mail system configuration
- General information about associated systems
- Operator desks
  - Desk features
  - Centralizing the operators
  - Operator desk structure
  - Operator desk structure diagram
- Traffic measurement system
- Billing system
  - Physical description
  - Logical description
  - Individual codes and cost centers
- PBXs management systems (small and large)
- Automatic calls distributors
- Contingency plan
- Subsystems interconnections
- Tables and spreadsheets

The items above cover most of the necessary information and should reflect the routing plan defined in the WAN design.

10.5 Documentation of All Contracted Resources (Dedicated and Switched)

The team in charge of coordinating the installation must prepare documentation indicating all resources contracted with the service providers, documenting where they are and how they are going to be interconnected to the equipment.

The team in charge of, for example, installing PBXs must have the list of all trunks to be connected to the equipment, including their IDs, locations in the wire distributors, and contacts of the service providers to execute tests. The documentation must indicate the resources per site. Never underestimate the importance of having a good inventory. You must be able to know what you have where and how much it costs and, of course, associate these resources to the people who need them. In other words, you must know what you manage and how much it costs. It is a somewhat basic thing to have. You may use inventory tools or even a simple paper list, whatever means you have. You cannot say you have any creditable management of telecommunications resources without even knowing what you have, where the resources are, and how much they cost.

10.6 Infrastructure Inventory and Documentation

The team responsible for coordinating the implementation should prepare a detailed inventory of resources to be installed and prepare diagrams of the physical installation to be executed. Such inventory must indicate each equipment, cable, and so forth. Associate each item to only one identifier, demonstrating how it is going to be installed in each site. Such detailing must indicate where each piece of equipment will be installed and how each connection (equipment and telco circuits) will be physically installed.

Keep in mind that the documentation may include things that are not present in the inventory, like plants, drawings, manuals, and so forth. In fact, the inventory is a part of the documentation. It is an important part, but still just a part.

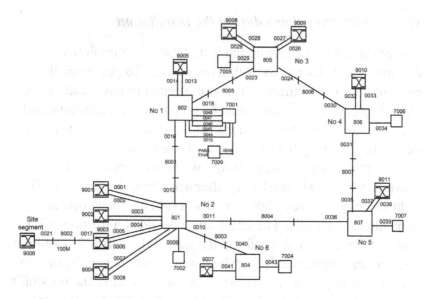

As can be seen in the picture above, each router, WAN switch, PBX, and cable has a specific identifier. This strategy guarantees the different assembling teams do not make mistakes and work in a coordinated way. Each site has to have a physical diagram as follows.

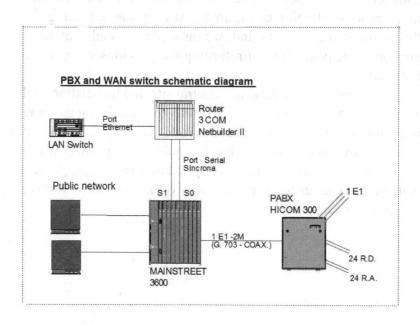

10.7 Contingency Plans during the Installation

One of the aims of planning the installation is to minimize disruption and risk to production operations. To guarantee the continuity of the connectivity, it is important to have contingency plans in place. These plans must be prepared and communicated in such way that the teams in charge of the installation are very well versed in what they have to do in each scenario.

In a migration of a large WAN, we never deactivate the previous structure immediately after activating the new one. The right strategy is to keep both structures (old and new) operating in parallel for a while. The exact time depends on the migration time, which, in turn, depends on the size of the network. Until the installation is concluded, the whole new structure may be unstable. In case of a large general failure, it is crucial to have the possibility of retuning everything as before. This kind of risk gets bigger as we move up in the OSI model. A leased line structure may be treated entirely on a one-by-one basis.

It is crucial that the team responsible for coordinating the installation of the new structure understand that, even if the connectivity of a specific site was activated, the new structure in the process of being configured is still unstable. Having this intrinsic fragility in mind, we must plan in such way to guarantee the possibility of returning the previous state, if so required.

For example, when having a central site, the installation of the equipment should be installed in parallel to the existing gateway maintaining the PVCs of the old network, working and configured as secondary routes. The new PVCs would be the primary route; the former one would be the secondary. Following strategies like that, we can guarantee the connectivity even if the new structure presents problems.

Transition schematic

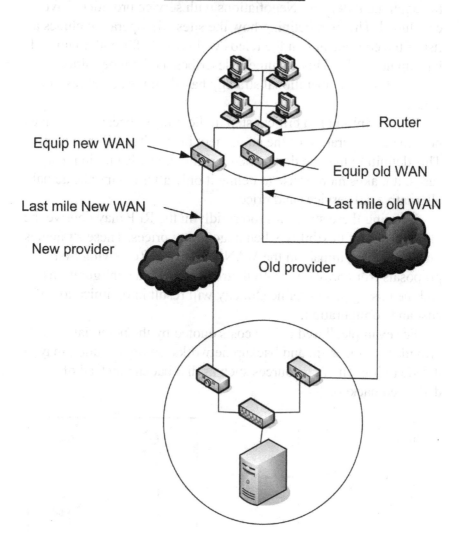

The strategy described is not the only possible strategy. Several others can be adopted from the simplest ones (manual change of cables) to sophisticated routing or switching strategies. The ideal situation varies in each case. The important point is that the team in charge of the project knows the risks well and foresees strategies to avoid interruption of the services.

10.8 Definition of How the Site Will Operate

At this point, we already have the backup strategy and models of the equipment defined. Negotiations with service providers have concluded. The plan defining how the sites will operate includes a list of the equipment that the telcos will provide for both main and backup networks. This document describes the final definitions/ details of the site operational strategy based on the actual resources contracted.

This definition is a critical step in the process because it defines how the configuration of the equipment in the sites will be exactly. This definition may be done when writing the RFP, but, in most cases, it makes more sense to define it only after having the actual alternatives of services and prices.

Defining these strategies too rigidly in the RFP may deprive the organization of flexibility when negotiating prices. These strategies may have a big impact in the WAN final price. Reviewing first proposals from providers with their coverage and configurations and then using this to refine strategy will result in optimization of cost and configuration.

For example, based on the costs quoted by the potential providers of the main and backup networks, an organization may decide to implement resources such as dial backup instead of dedicated backup.

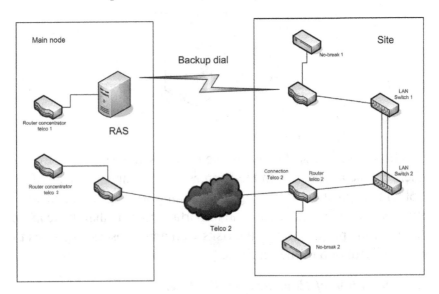

In another example, based on the cost of the backup link, an organization may decide to transport voice through these links. In this scenario, the switching mechanisms should be carefully configured to redirect the voice flow through the public network and the data flow to the backup in case of problems with the main link.

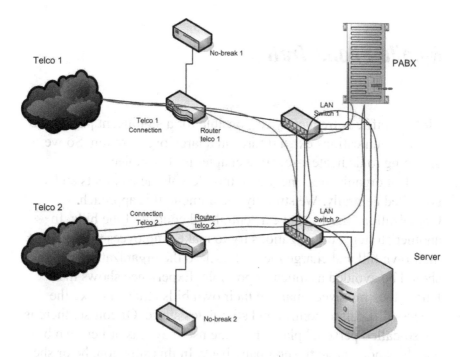

In the example above, the telco device 1 should be able to identify if the telco 2 fails. When it happens, it should receive and redirect the traffic. In this scenario where the routers belong to the telco, you will have to negotiate the direct interconnection between them. Most service providers refuse or resist such arrangements. In this scenario, the flow of voice should be blocked and redirected through the public network by the PBX.

Another important point when defining the strategy is guaranteeing that the backup network has real redundancy. So it does not make any sense to install two routers, but concentrate the access in only one LAN switch or only one no-break.

11

Mobile Phone Traffic

Mobile traffic is frequently responsible for a significant part of the telecommunications expenditures in a large organization. So we are going to dedicate a separate chapter to this subject.

Most organizations negotiate mobile volume contracts and are billed centrally. We strongly recommend this approach. Organizations need to have a centralized control of the bills. In another strategy, organizations try to make employees manage their own bill and charge the cost back to the organization. This should be avoided as much as possible. Experience shows that letting the employees manage their own bills tends to make the process difficult to control and stimulates abuse. Of course, there is the so-called personal plan where the user pays his or her own bill and does not charge the company back. In this situation, he or she is part of the group with the sole objective to get discounts when calling to or receiving calls from the organization. At this point, it is important to understand that the term *mobile traffic* means two different types of traffic:

- Traffic between fixed lines and mobiles phones
- Traffic between the mobile phones themselves

11.1 Traffic between Fixed Lines and Mobile Phones

The traffic between fixed lines and mobile phones is the traffic originated by the organization's voice trunks destined for mobile phones. In most countries, the cost of this kind of call is usually bigger than the regular calls between fixed-line phones and, in most cases, bigger than calls between mobile lines.

To identify the cost involved in accessing mobile phones from the organization's trunks, we need to analyze the organization's call logs and separate them between the fixed-to-mobile and fixed-to-fixed calls. Once we identify all calls originated by the organization whose destination was a mobile phone, we can understand what can be done to reduce this cost. It is possible to configure the PBXs to redirect calls destined for mobile phones to specific trunks. When redirecting the calls destined for mobile phones to specific trunks, it becomes possible to negotiate with the service provider's differentiated tariffs for this kind of call.

Another interesting strategy, which may be worth it in case you do not manage to get an adequate price for the fixed-to-mobile calls, is to install mobile trunks in the PBX ports in such way that we transform a call from fixed-to-mobile to a mobile-to-mobile.

This strategy will make sense only when the cost of the spoken minute in a mobile-to-mobile call is cheaper than the cost of the spoken minute for fixed-to-mobile. In this scenario, it becomes economically attractive to install mobile trunks in the PBX ports and reroute all fixed-to-mobile calls though these trunks. Nevertheless, it is important to keep in mind that this is not always true and everything depends on the negotiated cost of the spoken minute. When analyzing this alternative, we also have to consider the fact that the mobile trunks' adapters also have an associated cost.

To identify how many and where the mobile trunks are necessary to support the fixed-to-mobile traffic, we have to identify the number of calls, the duration, and cost of this kind of traffic in each site. Another important factor to be verified is the identification of the numbers (mobiles) to where the calls are destined. A relatively small quantity of numbers usually respond to a significant percentage of the calls. These numbers typically belong to employees, suppliers and relatives of the employees. They are natural candidates to be included into a corporate mobile tariff plan.

In case we manage to get differentiated tariffs among the mobile phones contracted by the organization (intra-org mobile traffic),[13] we should deploy mobile trunks in the PBXs to originate calls to mobile phones. Some mobile operators may object to this strategy for fear that, if the service used is linked with a PBX, it may be classified by the regulator as fixed-line service. Therefore, different sets of rules apply.

Usually providing a mobile number to employees' relatives and suppliers also reduces the cost of the service. When we do that, the organization starts paying a lot less, sometimes nothing, when calling the people they talk to the most. The mobile service providers usually have plans where the person using the phone receives the bill directly. The organization would not reimburse these users. The only benefit for them would be paying less to talk with the organization.

In addition to savings realized from the tariff plan adopted and usage profile, large savings may be achieved from avoiding roaming fees. It sometimes makes sense to use the mobile phone network for long-distance calls, even when comparing with the fixed-line tariffs. It is also possible and sometimes feasible to use the mobile phone trunks to provide communication among the organization's own sites.

11.2 Mobile-to-Mobile Traffic

Aggregated mobile traffic costs are often not visible to an organization and are frequently negotiated by purchasing teams within a large enterprise, not by the telecommunications area. Even when the negotiation team falls outside the telecommunications or IT function, they need to understand the possible solutions and get supporting documentation or analysis from the telecommunications area. We strongly recommend that the telecommunications team perform this kind of negotiation.

An organization in search of a better cost-benefit correlation for its mobile services should try to negotiate contracts with the service providers and stipulate differentiated tariffs, that is,

---

13   It is usual to get free traffic among the group.

differentiated in this context compared with the values adopted to the general public. Three sets of tariffs are usually negotiated:

- **Corporate mobiles:** Mobiles whose bills are paid directly by the organization.
- **Personal/business mobiles:** Mobiles whose bills are paid directly by the user, even though the organization may be coresponsible and the costs totally or partially expensed. This should be considered the same as corporate mobiles. We believe this strategy should be avoided, or a consolidated organization-wide bill should also be forwarded to the telecommunications area by the telco for validation.
- **Personal mobiles:** Mobiles whose bills are paid directly by the user but included as an option under the corporate contract. These are typically extended to family members of staff. The costs of these numbers are not reimbursable.

The organization usually gets two or three different sets of tariffs for the three types, and the tariffs typically contemplate four types of values with each one including local and long distance, as shown in the following picture.

Corporate mobiles	Cost per minute
Mobile to fix (local)	
Mobile to fix (long distance)	
Mobile to mobile on-net (local)	
Mobile to mobile on-net (long distance)	
Mobile to mobile off-net (local)	
Mobile to mobile off-net (long distance)	
Intra-group (local)	
Intra-group (long distance)	
Data services	
SMS service	

Personnal Mobiles	Cost per minute
Mobile to fix (local)	
Mobile to fix (long distance)	
Mobile to mobile on-net (local)	
Mobile to mobile on-net (long distance)	
Mobile to mobile off-net (local)	
Mobile to mobile off-net (long distance)	
Intra-group (local)	
Intra-group (long distance)	
Data services	
SMS service	

Telulares (mobile used in PBXs)	Cost per minute
Mobile to fix (local)	
Mobile to fix (long distance)	
Mobile to mobile on-net (local)	
Mobile to mobile on-net (long distance)	
Mobile to mobile off-net (local)	
Mobile to mobile off-net (long distance)	
Intra-group (local)	
Intra-group (long distance)	
Data services	
SMS service	

intra-group	Cost per minute
Intra-Group personnal	

It is not unusual to find pricing models where charges are applied per call or where there is a pool of minutes, that is, x amount of minutes free of charge per trunk per month. If you can, try to keep it as simple as possible. Avoid free franchises, which tend to hide the real cost of the spoken minute, and discounts applied separately. This makes the verification of the real amount difficult. Another option is to pool all minutes of the organization and, in that way, reduce the impact of graduated pricing models.

It is very important to map the destination of the calls and identify the average amount of minutes on- and off-net and, of course, on-net intragroup. Providers are much more flexible to offer discounts to calls within their own networks, and you should be able to take advantage of this situation.

The typical expectation, depending on the volume, is to get a reduced intragroup tariff, which is frequently zero in some jurisdictions, and eliminate any additional fee for national roaming and differentiated values when buying handsets and accessories.

Given all the different possibilities, the team requesting quotes should have accurate statistics to articulate the organization's requirements in terms of spoken minutes (with traffic interest and traffic matrix), handsets, volume estimates in spoken minutes of the corporate and personal groups, and data transfer requirements. This should also include the number of people who will be part of the personal group and how many handsets would be required.

The telecommunications manager preparing a RFP to contract mobile services should pay attention to the following general guidelines:

- The provider must be properly authorized by the regulator to provide the services and be completely in conformity with the pertinent national and state legislation.
- The service must be provided and charged on monthly basis and should not be subject to a contract exceeding thirty-six months.
- The users must be responsible for all incurred expenses on the personal phones.
- The provider must provide national coverage or, depending on the organization's state coverage, within and outside the

organization's buildings. The organization must evaluate the need (or not) for national coverage and, of course, inform the providers about the volume per area, for example, per state.

- The organization must decide, if appropriate, what kind of wireless multimedia services it requires, for example, Web browsing, text messages, e-mail, and so forth.
- It is recommended that the contract be directly between the organization and service provider itself, avoiding middlemen.
- The service provider must be able to provide a management tool through which reports and invoices can be attained.
- The service provider must be able to provide integration with SMS and e-mail services.
- The service provider must be able to provide high-speed access to special devices such as BlackBerry, detailing the associated charges.
- The mobile service should include the following associated services: call waiting, call forwarding, voice mail, conference, redial, ability to receive e-mails, data access, and caller ID.
- The service provider should be able to offer a wide range of alternatives in terms of handsets and accessories:
  - As an option, insurance can be offered in case of loss, theft, or damage.
  - The handsets should be able to automatically connect to an analog network where the digital ones are not available. This requirement depends on the country.
  - The mobile phones offered must include several vendors and models.

Resources such as capacity to limit the monthly traffic volume per mobile trunk are also very valuable, although not all service providers usually offer them. The possibility to limit the traffic volume is an important factor to mitigate the risk of default for the personal mobiles.

Usually, the cost-benefit attainable through reduced tariffs (or even zero cost) among the mobiles belonging to the corporate and personal groups (among the corporate and personal groups themselves and between the two groups) compensate many times for possible defaults by the users of the personal group. Such risk is even more reduced when volume limitations are introduced. In some circumstances, the organization may even manage to deduct the defaulted value from the payment owed to the employee whose relative defaulted the bill.

All these strategies depend on each organization's specific mobile traffic profile, but it is safe to assume that analyzing the traffic properly, adopting the strategies described, and using these strategies and studies to negotiate with the providers will tend to achieve very good results.

Finally, geographic location becomes very important when international calling is an important factor. Costs, services, and charging strategies for mobile services vary greatly between various countries.

In some countries, usually in small office environments, it sometimes makes financial sense to get rid of fixed-line services altogether. In other cases, international providers may be offering favorable rates in high-cost countries due to relationships and wholesale agreements. This is sometimes a strategy of offsetting costs in some emerging markets by leveraging overall spending in other jurisdictions.

12

Billing Auditing

The billing systems that the PTTs (public telephone and telegraph companies) use are typically large and complex applications. This complexity usually generates a lack of flexibility, resulting in errors in the telco bills. Verifying detailed, large corporate bills is not an easy task. Large organizations can have thousands of bills, each one having thousands of logs. Few companies can dedicate the time and effort necessary to properly analyze this huge amount of data.

Despite the complexity analyzing, verifying the bills is a necessity. Verification identifies charge discrepancies and enables the organization to get the due reimbursement for overcharging from the PTT providers. Experience shows that savings around 5 to 12 percent are usually attainable through regularly auditing the bills. Considering the expenditures with telecommunications of large organizations, even 5 percent means an enormous amount of money.

The auditing process usually requires having the bills in some electronic format. Assignment of resources to the review, solid contracts, and sound auditing procedures are requirements for auditing. Auditing will generally start showing financial results within ninety to one hundred and twenty days from the start of the procedure. Besides the direct financial gains, this kind of analysis enables the evaluation of many other important aspects linked with the management of a voice network:

- Identify limits when having exclusivity agreements is a valid alternative.
- Identify volumes at which having flat-rate contracts is a valid alternative.
- Determine at which point least cost route configuration in the PBXs needs adjustment.
- Determine when it becomes feasible to have a private voice network.
- Identify when using services such as CENTREX becomes feasible.
- Accurately calculate the number of trunks and circuits.

Analyzing the voice bills enables accurate answers to all these questions. The telecommunications manager should be aware that the analysis of a telecommunications bill is much more than just checking the tariffs. It is also about verifying the traffic and comparing the current prices against available alternatives. The process of verifying a bill usually follows these steps:

- Verify from and to where each call was made.
- Identify the area codes from and to each call.
- Based on the organization's specific contract, verify how much each call is supposed to cost and identify the discrepancies.
- Verify if the charging period is correct and if any additional fee is being charged for unsolicited services.
- Identify resources not in use; for example, trunks without any calls.
- Identify if the taxes were properly applied.

When auditing telephone bills it is important to consider the fact that this procedure is effective only when there is a process in place to define how and when the organization will be reimbursed.

12.1 Prerequisites

Having a process is only one prerequisite to effective auditing. The contract negotiation determines most of the criteria that makes auditing financially rewarding. Contracts must have dispute clauses. Ideally, the contracts in place should foresee that, if errors were spotted in the bills before the payment due date, the organization can notify the service provider and pay only what was considered due. The values over which there is disagreement must be discussed jointly. If the charges prove to be right, the organization pays the service provider without penalties for delaying the payment.

The organization must define a formal process through which all invoice disputes are done. This process needs a definition of time frames for each party involved and should be reflected in the dispute resolution clauses of individual contracts or master agreements. The whole process of disputing a bill from identification to solution typically should not exceed three months.

The SLA must consider that the invoice payment does not imply an acceptance of the charged values. The organization should have at least one year to audit the values charged.

Ideally, the SLA should foresee that, if errors identified exceed 5 percent of the total value of the bills, the service providers must reimburse the costs involved in auditing the bills to the organization. This is a considerable cost and a good mechanism for keeping service providers honest.

The organization must clearly define the time after which charges are not acceptable. For instance, the organization may include in the contract that services provided more than six months ago and not charged will not be paid. The organization must define a regular schedule of meetings with the service provider's invoice team. Such meetings would be a forum to discuss problems with the invoices and items added, changed, and canceled. The organization should try to define standardized invoice cycles and guarantee all invoices are due on the same day. This simplifies the billing and payment process.

Of course, all these recommendations depend on the negotiations at the contract stage. Arguably, these points belong in the negotiations chapter. However, these clauses only become meaningful if actual billing verification is done. Without it, you will have no recourse or knowledge of billing errors.

13

Applicability and Cases

In this chapter, we discuss the several situations where the techniques described in this book can be useful. We discuss real cases. We do not disclose the names of the organizations involved. We limit ourselves to indicating the type of service they provide. The cases were tailored to avoid even indirect identification of the organizations involved. In general, the beneficiaries can be grouped as follows:

- Large corporations with widely spread presence, including governments
- Venture capital companies that finance start-up telecommunications providers
- Call centers operators, including in-house operations and outsourcers
- Integrated solutions providers and telecommunications outsourcers
- Telecommunications service providers
- Hardware vendors
- IT consulting companies

Cases are presented in this chapter for each of these areas of applicability. Typically, organizations with points of presence spread throughout a large area with integrated operations or deploying some sort of call center service are the ones that can benefit the most from the techniques described in this book. In the cases presented for each one of the described types, we also demonstrate typical situations where such techniques can be particularly useful:

- When an organization is reevaluating its telecommunications cost factors
- When an organization is implementing new corporate systems with high telecommunications demands
- When an organization is deciding to outsource its telecommunications infrastructure or not
- When a call center service provider is analyzing the feasibility of implementing a new service (pricing a new service)
- When an organization is reevaluating its call center structure and trying to minimize its costs and establish a clear correlation between services/volume/cost and revenue
- When two organizations are merging

The techniques of mapping network traffic and planning and implementing a WAN can help each type of organization listed above. This section illustrates applicability to each situation with a case. We describe the typical contexts where design or redesign of the WAN using algorithms becomes important.

13.1 Large Corporations with Widespread Presence (Government Included)

Large organizations with widespread geographical presence and integrated services rely heavily on telecommunications. Consequently, these types of organizations benefit the most from the techniques described here. Telecommunications usually represent a large percentage of their IT budget, usually only surpassed by personnel. So identifying a savings of as little as 5 percent in a large corporate network can amount to tens of thousands of dollars per month. Initially, we are going to describe a project developed by a large bank in Brazil where we had a situation very typical.

13.1.1 Large Organization Reevaluates Its WAN Using Design Tools

This case involved a bank with fifteen thousand employees and eight hundred points of presence (two hundred and twenty-two branches and five hundred and seventy-eight sub-braches) distributed across the south and southeast of Brazil. The monthly telecommunications expenditures were US$1.15 million.

The bank had a SNA data processing structure based on two mainframes located at its headquarters in Porto Alegre. The corporation did not have any kind of voice and data integration. Both media had completely different transport strategies. The data network had a completely centralized star topology. Voice was transported through the PSTNs. The data circuits contracted were dedicated point-to-point circuits.

The interconnection alternatives were three nationwide carriers (IXCs) and three regional RBOCs. Nevertheless, by law, only the nationwide carriers could provide the interconnection between states outside of their regions. The carriers included:

Nationwide	EMBRATEL
	EQUANT
	COMSAT
Regional Carriers	TELEMAR
	TELEFONICA
	BRASIL TELECOM

The bank was going through difficult times so it had to come up with every possible strategy to reduce its operational costs. The prices paid for the telecommunications resources were very much in line with what was typical, so there was little room for the kick-the-telco strategy. Besides, time was a critical constraint. Any saving initiative could not extrapolate six months (actual savings reflecting in the cash flow).

Faced with this dilemma, the IT management decided to invest some effort in redesigning the network. The objective was to spot opportunities of savings that were not obvious. The drive to think the network better and deploy algorithms was taken only due to extreme pressure, not conscious planning. In fact, the IT management, faced with the need to produce savings and aware that kicking the telco even more was not feasible, was forced to rethink the whole network structure. It is like getting to the alternative of planning the network better by force, not conviction. Once the analysis was done, it became clear that savings were attainable from two main sources: voice and data integration (internal calls and long distance flowing through the network) and topological rearrangements.

Mapping the traffic and using design tools identified that a much more cost-effective structure could be achieved with an eleven-node topology integrating the internal calls between these nodes and carrying the long-distance calls to the nearest node:

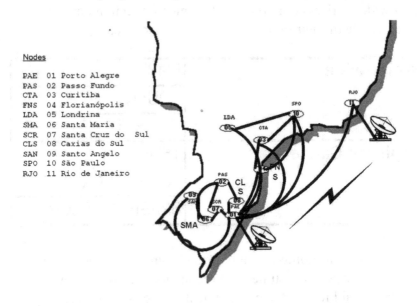

Nodes

PAE 01 Porto Alegre
PAS 02 Passo Fundo
CTA 03 Curitiba
FNS 04 Florianópolis
LDA 05 Londrina
SMA 06 Santa Maria
SCR 07 Santa Cruz do Sul
CLS 08 Caxias do Sul
SAN 09 Santo Angelo
SPO 10 São Paulo
RJO 11 Rio de Janeiro

The economical and operational results were outstanding. The rearrangement of the structure managed to reduce the monthly expenditures by almost 50 percent, from US$1,151,061 to US$681,654. Despite the cost reduction, the network capacity was increased by almost three times, and its resilience was enhanced with backups for all nodes.

Situation before the Implementation

Type of service	Monthly cost US$
Outside network PSTN calls	592.231,30
Telex	26.978,00
Data circuits	531.852,00
Total	**1.151.061,30**

Situation after the Implementation

Type of service	Monthly cost US$
Access	379.429,00
Backbone	114.294,00
Hardware	55.000,00
Telex	26.976,00
Outside network PSTN calls	105.960,00
Total	**681.654,00**

In this particular case, the savings were achieved doing a better network design and integrating voice into the data network, transporting the long-distance calls through the private data channels. The use of design tools made it possible to generate the voice traffic matrixes and identify where to concentrate traffic and how to transport the flows. Just to illustrate, the organization had almost seven million calls per month. It identified the percentage of these calls that were internal (30 percent) and the interest of traffic per area code. Without tools, it would be very hard to transform this amount of raw data in usable information and even harder to simulate operational scenarios (topologies and alternatives of services), not to mention identify the best structure. All the planning was executed within a month, and the actual implementation was within five months. This particular case demonstrates two things:

- Thinking the network better pays off even when there is no room for negotiating prices for the services.

119

- The telecommunications teams and IT managers tend to resist whole rearrangements. They usually only accept that when they have no choice. Another important factor here was the time constraint, which, by itself, forced the use of analytical tools.

This case also shows us that the internal team sometimes has the strong conviction that they are doing the best possible job,[14] and there is not any possibility for improvement. Tools allow us to treat the huge amount of data, transforming it into information and allowing us to see savings opportunities.

13.1.2 State Government Revaluates Its Telecommunications Infrastructure

In this case, each government agency had the autonomy to contract and manage its own telecommunications infrastructure independently. This strategy, although generating operational flexibility, was clearly generating higher costs. Faced with these several separated networks, the government decided a whole planning was necessary.

The organization itself was composed of seventy-two agencies and state-owned companies having fifteen hundred sites with approximately eighty thousand employees spread all over the state. The monthly telecommunications budget, including voice and data, was US$2.0 million. There was some voice integration within some of the agencies, but, for the most part, voice and data had different transport strategies.

There was a perception that, negotiating as only one large organization, the state government would be the biggest client for any of the telcos operating within the state. That would increase its leverage over them and generate the possibility of achieving substantial discounts. So, in this example, there was room for negotiable savings. Thinking the network as only one large organization would also allow the identification of the locations where more than one state agency occupied the same address,

---

14   And, as in this example, from the negotiational perspective, they were.

avoiding the need for multiple circuits serving the same address and, therefore, reducing costs.

The state already had an IT services company, which the state completely owned. This centralized the data processing for the main agencies, even though some agencies and state-controlled companies had their own data centers. This company was the natural option to assume the telecommunications centralization process.

This context as a whole convinced the government management to properly plan the telecommunications structure; size of the organization and need for quick results was what forced the use of analytical tools.

This is a case where data gathering was very painful. It happened because it was necessary to map the location of each address of each government agency and get the telephone bill of each trunk and circuit connected to each address. All this had to be done in a very politically sensitive environment where some agencies were very jealous of their telecommunications network and participating in the process halfheartedly. In addition, the telcos involved also did everything they could to delay the process because they knew nothing good could come from it to them.

A team of twenty people managed to put all the data together in approximately three months, which, considering the issues described, was a quite good performance. The facts of the organization were as follows:

- Fifteen hundred POPs distributed throughout seventy-two agencies and nine hundred and seventy-eight addresses.
- Nearly eighty-three thousand workstations.
- Six hundred and fifty-seven sites with dedicated circuits. Among them there were two hundred whose connectivity was already provided by the state's IT provider company (approximately 30 percent of the total), facilitating even more the centralization process.
- The fact that the state's IT provider already owned over nine thousand of the workstations currently in use by the state (11 percent of the workstations being used).

As soon the bills were consolidated and treated by a design tool, several interesting things appeared. The information uncovered in the analysis was the following:

- The fifteen hundred government POPs were located into nine hundred and seventy-eight addresses. Only thirty-two of these were main addresses.
- Five hundred and twenty-two POPs were located in addresses where at least one other government POP was located. That by itself opened the possibility of reducing the number of data circuits and voice trunks.
- Fixed-to-mobile calls represented almost 40 percent of all voice telecommunications cost.
- The trunk subscriptions represented 15 percent of the voice telecommunications costs.
- Almost 60 percent of the fixed-to-fixed traffic was internal (between the government itself), and 80 percent of it occurred between the thirty-two main addresses.

Through analyzing the traffic, it became clear that integrating voice and data between the state main administrative centers would generate savings of thousands of dollars because most voice traffic was among the agencies themselves. Without a centralized management, none would take the initiative of building a private WAN or MAN or integrating voice. That finding reinforced the need for planning the network centralized. The cost structure identified was as follows:

Type of service	Monthly cost US$
Local mobile	USD 816.557,87
Frame-relay circuits	USD 488.443,67
Local Calls	USD 244.195,60
Trunks subscriptions	USD 336.664,81
Mobile long distance	USD 7.899,31
Long distance calls	USD 15.664,23
Mobile international	USD 1.415,16
TOTAL	USD 1.910.840,67

It was identified that the savings would come from six main sources:

- Massive deployment of mobile trunks in the state's PBXs that would transform the cost from fixed-to-mobile to mobile-to-mobile[15]
- A renegotiation with the state's main telco, bringing the costs of the data network down approximately 60 percent
- A merge in the circuits installed in the same addresses, reducing the number of necessary circuits by almost 40 percent
- An improvement in the internal controls, avoiding unnecessary expenses and allowing a better management
- A renegotiation of the voice contracts, bringing down the current costs by approximately 30 percent
- An integration of voice and data between the state's main sites, eliminating almost 60 percent of the voice traffic

All these initiatives allowed a monthly saving of 57 percent of the current expenditures, as shown through the spreadsheet below:

Type of service	Monthly cost	Monthly savings %	Monthly savings (USD)
mobile calls (local)	USD 816,557.87	60.72%	USD 495,813.94
Frame-relay Circuits	USD 488,443.67	76.00%	USD 371,217.19
Local Calls	USD 244,195.60	60.00%	USD 146,517.36
Trunks Subscriptions	USD 336,664.81	25.00%	USD 84,166.20
Mobile calls (Long distance)	USD 7,899.31	41.91%	USD 3,310.39
Long distance calls	USD 15,664.23	15.00%	USD 2,349.63
Mobile Calls International	USD 1,415.16	90.57%	USD 1,281.78
TOTAL	USD 1,910,840.67	57.81%	USD 1,104,656.50

This is a classical example where a combined set of initiatives (technical, administrative, and negotiational), when applied together, can have a huge impact on the overall telecommunications expenditures. The combination of better management, including a thorough resources mapping with a detailed analysis using tools and an intense negotiation, managed to save the government US$1.1 million per month. Mapping the resources and deploying design tools was instrumental to the following initiatives:

---

15   In Brazil's tariff system, this meant a reduction of almost 45 percent in the cost of the minute.

- **Rationalization of mobile traffic:** The huge weight of the mobile phone traffic in the overall expenditures and the identification that 60 percent of the fixed telephone traffic was between the organization's own sites.
- **Consolidation of negotiation process:** The consolidation of all resources contracted allowed the organization to present itself to the service providers as only one entity, leveraging its capacity of getting better deals.
- **Share of resources:** Data circuits were consolidated per address. Before, an address had data circuits dedicated to each one of the government agencies located there.
- **Deployment of a private backbone:** Through this analysis, the feasibility of having a private voice and data network interconnecting the government main addresses was clear. Such a network was built in a record time and within less than six months. All the savings planned were effective.

The techniques described in this book gave the state's management a clear view of what had to be done and why, allowing the identification of which economic benefit was associated with each initiative.

13.1.3 A Mexican Financial Organization Looks for Alternatives to Achieve Telecommunications Cost Reductions

This case took place in a financial service provider that employed around forty-two hundred people in its one hundred and sixty-five Mexican branches. A series of problems related to the network reliability, performance, and cost convinced management to reevaluate the situation. The drive to analyze the network did not come from the IT department, but from above, the financial director who somehow figured out that the organization was expending more than its competitors with telecommunications.

The first step was to do a detailed inventory of all telecommunications resources and a detailed study of voice and data traffic. It was a relatively easy process given the fact that the telecommunications area in this respect was very well organized. Once it was done, design tools were deployed to map the voice and data traffic and identify what we could define as the ideal theoretical network. The current cost distribution was as follows:

Service Provider	Monthly value
TELMEX	USD 633.575,95
TELCEL	USD 51.141,00
AT&T	USD 177.951,68
AVAYA	USD 134.059,60
GNS International Links	USD 24.583,65
Other operational expenses	USD 125.447,00
TOTAL	**USD 1.146.758,88**

The deployment of design tools allowed the identification of the traffic intraorganization (the internal voice traffic matrix), the outbound traffic profile (traffic matrix), and, of course, the study of several possible scenarios. All these analyses gave the management a clear view of what could be done and why, allowing the identification of which economic benefit was associated with each initiative.

As can be seen in the picture below, the data network had a star topology with Mexico City as its center. There was some voice integration among the five main sites: three of them within Mexico City itself and the other two at Monterrey and Guadalajara.

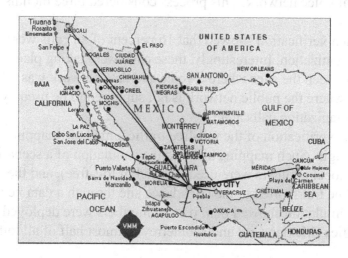

Thoroughly analyzing the traffic, the interconnection costs available, and other associated costs (hardware, maintenance, and operation), the design tools identified that the network could be costing around US$920,000 monthly. It was almost 20 percent less than the current expenditures. The data gathering and analysis followed the steps described in this book and was conducted detailing the following traffics:

- Intraorganization traffic
- Toll-free voice traffic (48 percent of all voice expenditures)
- Fixed traffic (local, long-distance, and international) (25 percent of all voice expenditures)
- Fixed-to-mobile traffic (27 percent of all voice traffic)
- Data network structure (traffic interest, profile, and volumes)

Initially, it verified all long-distance calls taken between the organization's own trunks (intraorganization traffic). That analysis consisted of crossing the organization trunks file with the calls log file (CDR) (1,200 trunks × 1.5 million calls). Doing that, we managed to extract all intraorganization calls, identifying the volume, cost, and traffic matrix intraorganization. This cost was the cost that would be absorbed by an integrated voice and data network and is the reference to any cost-benefit analysis of an only internal voice network. This process considered three months as a reference.

Such verification showed that 16 percent of all calls were intraorganization. Interestingly, these calls were taking place also between the sites where a voice and data network was in place, where the public network is not supposed to be used by intraorganization calls at all.

The verification of the toll-free traffic aimed the mapping of calls origin. Such mapping allowed the simulation of a scenario where local numbers were used (instead of toll-free), and the traffic would be transported to the attendance site through a data network. Such simulation showed that, if local numbers were deployed in two cities (Mexico City and Monterrey), almost half of all toll-free cost would be transferred to the callers. This information was crucial when negotiating discounts with the provider.

Analyzing the mobile traffic, it was verified that 30 percent of it was overflowing the existent TELCEL trunk groups and flowing through the regular TELMEX public voice network, paying a tariff of almost 50 percent higher per spoken minute. The increase of the number of TELCEL trunks would bring the fixed-to-mobile cost down almost 50 percent overnight, that is, half of 27 to 13.5 percent of all voice costs.

Analyzing the international traffic showed that 90 percent of all calls were to countries covered by the existent voice and data network, so they were supposed to go through this network, not through the public network. It was verified that the PBXs were not properly configured and did not redirect the calls through the existent voice and data network. The simple and easy procedure of configuring the PBXs properly would bring the international cost almost to zero.

Analyzing the data network, it was verified that the network had two hundred and forty circuits connecting one hundred and sixty-five sites. One hundred were clear channels, and one hundred and forty were frame relay accesses. Regarding the data network, the following optimization possibilities were identified:

- Some addresses had redundant circuits (and some had more than nine) because each business unit had autonomy to contract its own circuits. The organization had five business units operating in Mexico.
- The oversubscription in Mexico City gateway (frame relay network) was one to ten. This fact demonstrated that the access bandwidth was overdimensioned and could be reduced by an average of 30 percent.
- High costs were associated with managing and maintaining the telecommunications hardware (paying two times the usual value).

In this case, a large part of the savings came not from rearranging things, but from properly deploying the resources already in place. As we can see, the organization already had a mobile plan and voice channels (national and international). By just mapping the traffic, it became possible to spot the problems, which were mostly linked with poor management/control over the resources.

Of course, a diligent verification of the bills could have identified some of these problems. However, the analysis of this huge amount of data monthly is a hard task. Even for a more sophisticated telecommunications department, it would have been difficult to spot things such as the internal traffic, although not the international and mobile ones.

The fact that different business units each had their own circuits is more of an administrative problem than anything. The complete mapping of the structure exposed the problem and its price, but the telecommunications department probably could have not done anything to prevent it from happening. At this point, the power to contract circuits belonged to the business units themselves, which may or may not inform back to the telecommunications area.

The deployment of design tools made possible the consolidation and treatment of the data. The analysis and simulations, which gave the management a clear view, made it possible to be seen what had to be done and why, allowing the identification of which economic benefit was associated with each initiative. All mapping and analytical work took two months. The implementation and actual savings took an additional three months to be achieved.

13.1.4 A Major South American Municipality Revaluates Its Telecommunications Infrastructure

A major South American city government reevaluated its telecommunications infrastructure, mapping the voice traffic and defining the telecommunications contracting policies. The drive for this project, as in our previous case, came from the financial side of the organization and against the will of all main actors, IT and telecommunications managers and providers. This seems to be a recurrent situation and may deserve some comments.

First, very often, the people directly involved with the telecommunications area tend to resist to this kind of reanalysis. They honestly believe that an analysis is not necessary or they fear that, if an analysis is done and optimization is found, it will look like they are not doing their job properly. In this sense, the analysis is seen as a threat to the status quo or undue intervention. In both situations, our experience shows that they are mistaken. If you are a telecommunications manager or IT manager and the initiative to reevaluate the network comes from outside, we strongly suggest you embrace it and make as if it were your own. It is a win-win situation. If savings are achieved, your actions were part of it. If they aren't, which is quite unusual, you will be seen as the one who was doing a good job and, nevertheless, always willing to improve.

This case was developed within a public organization and, as it is natural, a very politicized environment. The main objective of the analysis was the identification of savings opportunities and definition of the contracting strategy for each service. As in the state government case, each municipal agency had autonomy to contract and manage its own voice infrastructure independently, which provides flexibility but higher costs. On the data side, there was centralization.

The organization itself was composed of thirty-four agencies and municipal companies having more than thirty-three hundred sites with approximately one hundred and twenty thousand employees spread all over the city. The monthly telecommunications budget, including voice and data, was US\$3.5 million without any voice and data integration.

The voice traffic mapping demonstrated that 65.48 percent of the voice costs were due to calls between fixed trunks to mobile phones and only 27.68 percent were due to fixed-to-fixed trunks. In addition, it was verified that 42 percent of the fixed traffic was among the organization's own trunks, and 30 percent of this total was among just sixteen sites:

Number of sites	% of the intra-org traffic	Value to be absorbed by an private voice network
16	30,00%	USD 40.444,09
34	40,00%	USD 53.925,45
136	60,00%	USD 80.888,18
407	80,00%	USD 107.850,91
3223	100,00%	USD 134.813,63

Each address was identified and physically located, allowing the understanding that 80 percent of all addresses were located within the city's hyper-center where the availability of telecommunications providers was high. At least four alternatives were available. The mapping identified over thirty-two hundred points of presence distributed through thirty-four agencies located in more than three thousand addresses. The cost structure was as follows:

Type of service	Monthly cost	%
Calls to Mobile phones local (VC1)	USD 1.195.799,60	33,68%
Local calls	USD 357.522,28	10,07%
Long distance nationwide	USD 180.803,08	5,09%
Calls to Mobile phones long distance	USD 90.493,76	2,55%
International calls	USD 3.107,59	0,09%
Data circuits	USD 1.722.222,22	48,51%
Total	USD 3.549.948,54	100,00%

Understanding this reality, it became possible to define the telecommunications infrastructure policies and strategies. It was also possible to define the priorities among the several possible initiatives. These aspects became clear:

- Given the pattern of the geographical location of the sites, concentrated within the core of the city where several alternatives of service providers are available, the contracting policy should allow that parts of the network be contracted with different providers. This policy would be completely different than the actual one, where the provider must be able to provide all circuits. The actual policy eliminates all service providers but one. It was identified that competition would decrease the current circuit cost by at least 21 percent.

- There is the need to contract and control the voice network in a centralized way. Through that, the organization will be able to bring all its weight to the negotiation table and obtain better tariffs, including zero tariff for trunks subscription.
- The voice and data integration was economically feasible only among the sixteen main sites. The maximum gain from integrating voice would be around US$40,444 per month.
- The adoption of MPLS technology, replacing the existing frame relay network, would not be justifiable by the need for voice integration. It was an important conclusion because it forced the provider to recognize that the replacement of the frame relay network for MPLS was mostly due to its own needs, not a real benefit for the client. This conclusion had an immediate impact on the ongoing negotiations.

There was a perception that negotiating as only one large organization would increase its leverage over the service providers and generate the possibility of achieving substantial discounts. This strategy was already adopted regarding the data network. Operating the network as only one large organization would also allow the identification of the locations where more than one city's agency would occupy the same address, avoiding the need for multiple voice trunks and PBXs serving the same address and therefore reducing costs.

The city already had an IT services company that the city completely owned, centralizing the data processing and data network. This company was the natural option to assume the voice centralization process. It was identified that the savings would come from six main sources:

- Massive deployment of mobile trunks in the city's PBXs, which would transform the cost of fixed-to-mobile to mobile-to-mobile, which in this country's tariff system, meant a reduction of almost 33 percent in the cost of the spoken minute.

- Renegotiation with the actual main provider brought the data costs down between 21 and 40 percent.
- Merging the circuits, trunks, and PBXs that were installed in the same addresses reduced the number of necessary circuits by approximately 5 percent.
- Improving the internal controls avoided unnecessary expenses and allowed a better management.
- Renegotiating the voice contracts brought down the current costs with trunks subscription to zero.
- Voice and data was integrated among the sixteen city's main sites.

All these initiatives allowed a monthly saving of 26.24 percent of the current expenditures, as shown through the spreadsheet below:

Type of service	Current Monthly cost	Foresaw cost	% of savings identified	Savings
Calls to Mobile phones local (VC1)	USD 1.195.799,60	USD 797.199,73	33,33%	USD 398.599,87
Trunks monthly subscription	USD 134.324,44	USD 0,00	100,00%	USD 134.324,44
Local calls	USD 357.522,28	USD 329.744,50	7,77%	USD 27.777,78
Long distance nationwide	USD 180.803,08	USD 153.682,62	15,00%	USD 27.120,46
Calls to Mobile phones long distance	USD 90.493,76	USD 73.256,86	19,05%	USD 17.236,91
International calls	USD 3.107,59	USD 3.107,59	0,00%	USD 0,00
Data circuits	USD 1.722.222,22	USD 1.360.555,56	21,00%	USD 361.666,67
Total	USD 3.684.272,99	USD 2.717.546,86	26,24%	USD 966.726,12

The deployment of design tools made the analysis and simulations possible, which gave the city's management a clear view of what had to be done and why, allowing the identification of which economic benefit was associated with each initiative. All mapping and analytical work took two months. It is important to emphasize that, in an organization of this size, the deployment of tools is mandatory. There is no way to map and study the traffic manually.

In this project, we can easily recognize the topic discussed in chapter seven, where the obligation of providing all circuits practically eliminated the competition and brought the costs up. The IT manager/director must be very active in the definition of the contracting policy, preventing lower levels of the organization from taking this kind of decision and eliminating the possibility of undue advantage to any potential provider. Sometimes, due to these unhappy strategic decisions, the negotiation process is doomed even before beginning.

13.2 Venture Capital Companies that Finance Start-up Telecommunications Providers

Venture capitalist companies are one breed of companies that can benefit a lot from the techniques described in this book. These firms may invest in telcos or service providers of various sizes. These techniques are useful for the venture capital firm to model the operation of a start-up telecommunications service provider and identify the ideal structure to support a given traffic volume. Using analytical tools, it becomes possible to perform many calculations using several traffic volumes. Through these analyses, the correlation between volume and cost can be established. This is crucial information to define the necessary investment and expected revenue. It provides information on risk and return for many scenarios based on the likely growth of the financed telco.

The possibility of setting many volume scenarios allows the clear identification of how the infrastructure cost changes with the volumes transported. For instance, if we were analyzing a proposed service provider infrastructure, we could identify expenses and revenues per volume. In doing so, we can generate three curves:

- volume × infrastructure costs
- volume × operational costs
- volume × revenue

With this information, it is possible to identify the company cash flow and other aspects such as break-even point (minimum amount of traffic necessary to make a project feasible), ROI, and profitability per volume. In summary, it becomes possible to build the service provider business model, simulate all volume scenarios, and estimate the risk of the investment.

13.1.2 A Company Analyzes the Feasibility of Providing Telecommunications Services

This case involves a Canadian shopping mall real estate company with more than two hundred shopping centers across Canada. The company was trying to determine the feasibility of implementing a private voice and data network to be offered as part of its services to its tenants. Here it was necessary to execute a cost-benefit analysis to identify the correlation between the volume, costs, and possible revenues and evaluate if the necessary investment was worthwhile.

The company's management wanted to know if they could maximize their assets by offering additional telecommunications services to its tenants. The company's closest competitor had just started offering an integrated services package, including cabling, voice and data services, and premises equipment.

The deployment of analytical software allowed the simulation of several different volume scenarios. Through these simulations, it became possible to establish the correlation between volume and cost (investment and operational) and volume and revenue. It also made it possible to simulate several pricing strategies and values by analyzing the revenue using several pricing strategies for each volume.

The possibility to set many volume scenarios is extremely useful because it allows the visualization of how the infrastructure cost and revenues change depending on the volume transported or prices charged. So it becomes possible to produce a graphic correlating this grandness. For instance, in this particular case, when analyzing a service provider infrastructure (what the real estate company was going to become to its tenants), we were able to identify two curves:

- volume × infrastructure costs
- volume × revenue

With this information, we were able to identify the company cash flow and aspects like break-even point, ROI, and profitability per volume for each pricing strategy. In summary, we were able to build the service provider business model.

This study identified the minimum number of clients (voice and data traffic) necessary to make the network feasible and compared the costs involved (infrastructure and operation) with the possible rates chargeable from the tenants. The study showed that the company had to convince at least 40 percent of its tenants to use the service in order to make it feasible. It was not that simple though because the major tenants (large retail stores) represented just 35 percent of the total number of tenants. So the company had to convince all the major tenants and at least 5 percent of the smaller retail stores to use the new services. After this break-even point, the profitability curve would grow smoothly.

But most of the major retailers already had their own network strategies and were unlikely to implement different strategies just for the stores located inside the company's malls. Furthermore, most small retailers (60 percent) did not need this kind of service because they did not have a very wide geographical dispersion or large number of points of presence.

The curve below shows how the revenues and operational costs behave in this specific case:

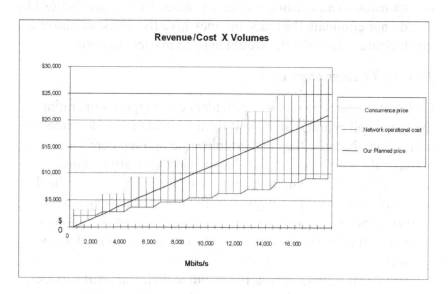

The superior curve shows the current costs paid by the clients today. The inferior curve shows the operational costs of the network, and the central curve shows the revenue assuming a given price strategy to be adopted. The X of the graphic shows the volume in megabits, and the Y is the value in USD. As we can see clearly, adopting a price strategy where the price charged by the company would be around 30 percent below the competition, which is necessary to motivate the tenants to move from the current provider, we would need at least 3,000 megabits to break even, crossing of the grey curve with the dark grey curve. This does not count the value of the necessary investment. As we can see, after 3,000 megabits, the operational profit grows as the volume grows. Of course, this curve uses megabits as its X, but we could easily use percent of the potential market, which has a direct correspondence with the volume, indicating what would be the revenue and operational cost if we had a given percentage of the market. Another interesting thing not demonstrated in this graphic is the fact that the simulators can calculate the cost of the investment for each volume and demonstrate it at the top of the operational costs as long we define an amortization time and interest rate. All this makes the planning of a new service provider or expansion of an existing one much easier. Of course, studies like that do not eliminate the risks, but they give the decision-maker a much clearer view of what would happen in each scenario.

13.3 Call Center Operators

Call center operators (service providers or enterprises operating their own call center) can benefit from the techniques described in this book because they can establish the optimal correlation between the user's geographical dispersion, its traffic volume/flows, and tariff system, indicating exactly how they would be the ideal structure to support a given traffic originated/designated to a given population. This analysis can save an enormous amount of money in telco charges and help the companies to model new services.

Many call centers operators outsource their transport services, relying entirely on carriers to provide the interconnection between their clients and attendance sites. This strategy, although practical in operational terms, very often creates higher transport costs. Outsourcing the call transport entirely deprives the call centers operators of two fundamental possibilities of reducing operational costs:

- The toll-free contracts usually do not discriminate the origin of the calls, defining a flat rate per spoken minute (very often with discount per quantity) regardless from where the call was placed. Not having a distributed traffic capitation structure makes it impossible for the call center operator to take advantage of the tariff system by exploring different interconnection costs associated with the user's geographical distribution. For example, in Canada, the calls within the same area code are not charged. If you only have a toll-free number and are locked in a flat-rate contract, you will pay for the call even if most of your clients are calling from the same area code of your attendance site.
- If a call center operator does not have any capitation node, it cannot distribute its IVRs and cannot take advantage (in terms of transport costs) of the services whose process can be addressed by these devices, obligating all calls, including the ones going to the IVRs, to be transported all the way to the attendance sites.

The same concepts applicable to the organization using call centers themselves apply to a call center outsourcer. The gains attainable through this process can be transferred to the clients, making the call center provider more competitive in the market or allowing it to keep increasing its profitability.

So, if the call center operator decides to implement its own transport network, there is usually plenty of room for optimizations. But not any design will bring savings. An overengineered and poorly designed transport structure may become even expensive than an outsourced one. Consequently, the challenge is to design a structure that minimizes the costs involved with transporting the calls while maintaining the same high levels of service.

The magnitude of the savings achievable by implementing this strategy varies and is directly related to the geographical dispersion of the users. However, through the careful analysis of traffic flows, interconnection costs, and tariff rules, it is not unusual to find more than 50 percent savings in real dollar terms over today's transport costs.

Although the identification of an ideal structure to transport a given traffic volume is in itself already a huge benefit, further analysis can be done. The same process, which allows the calculation of these structures quickly, opens the door to working through many calculations using several traffic volumes. Through this analysis, it is possible to establish the correlation between volume and cost, as described in the previous topic.

Through this process, it is possible to identify the correlation between traffic volumes, infrastructure cost, and revenues as they relate to the services that the call centers offer. For example, assume the business is considering offering a new service as an additional service offering. The analysis enables the modeling of business cases identifying the correlation between each new service and the associated transport cost involved in implementing it effectively.

By providing such elaborate and accurate information to the business, this process becomes a powerful decision-support tool. It makes it possible to generate simulations where the break-even points are identified and shows how different volumes, topologies, technologies, or interconnection service providers influence the overall cost of the structures analyzed.

The tools produce all the project details: topology, equipment, trunks, backbone circuits, IVR distributions, paths, service providers, and number of attendants per shift. Consequently, having this clear view of what needs to be implemented and/or changed, we can construct the whole project plan, including phases and schedules. With a clear view of the effort necessary to adjust/implement the call center structure, we can decide how, when, or if the project will be implemented at all.

Having a dynamic model enables us to analyze how the variables involved influence each other and verify how changing each one of them affects the overall cost of the structure. These correlations allow the organization to make decisions with respect to a wide range of issues, from the purely technical to strategic. For example:

- Market strategies
  - The minimum amount of users necessary to make the services feasible
  - Services provided
  - How much is charged by each service

- Operational strategies
  - Who pays for the access (availability toll-free access or not)
  - If the organization will provide local numbers
  - If services are provided only through the IVRs, live attendants, or both
  - In or outsource of transport
  - Technical strategies
  - If to use traffic caption nodes
  - If to distribute the IVRs
  - Voice compression rate
  - Acceptable QoS
  - Hardware and interconnection providers
  - Interconnection technologies

Decisions like the ones mentioned above are very hard to make without an automated tool that analyzes all aspects of the issue. It becomes even harder when varying the demand that the call center is supposed to handle. The analysis provides the ability to make well-educated decisions, such as who pays for the access and which services will be offered only through the IVRs or only through live attendants. For instance, if we verify that 90 percent of our users are located inside the area codes of our nodes, we may consider the alternative of not providing toll-free services for these areas at all.

If we have an infrastructure already in place, we should compare the costs of the new call center with the actual one. At this point, it will become clear which cost factors in the actual structure could be reduced, and we can produce a very straightforward, high-level managerial report, comparing the actual expenditures with the proposed ones. With the results of this calculation, we can identify the cost of the proposed infrastructure and compare it with the actual cost. We can also calculate the savings and ROI of the project.

Having a clear view of how much it would cost to build its transport infrastructure, the organization better understands how much would be reasonable to pay for a completely outsourced transport solution. In addition, when soliciting bids for an outsourced solution, the process is again simplified because the parameters around the requirements are predefined and constant. This gives the organization the ability to compare apples to apples when reviewing the proposals. So it makes the evaluation process simple in this respect.

13.3.1 Financial Company Optimizes Its Call Center Transport Structure

This case describes a project where a worldwide-diversified financial services company analyzed its telecommunications infrastructure in its call center operations in Brazil.

- The total of spoken minutes per month was 4,519,676.
- The number of calls was 1,396,327.
- The average call duration was 3.23 minutes.
- All calls were handled by a call center located in Rio de Janeiro and originated from all parts of Brazil.
- It had a contract with one of Brazil's main ILECs (Telemar), paying a flat rate.
- The alternative of service providers available were EMBRATEL, TELEMAR, TELEFONICA, and INTELIG, all providing either dedicated or switched connections.
- In Brazil, the calls within the same area code are charged. The toll-free calls can be charged differently, depending on where they originated.

The company was studying alternatives to reduce its telecommunications costs. Studying the traffic uncovered an improved design possibility. Its research found these facts:

- The company's current telecommunications costs were US$828,000 per month.
- The redesigned structure of the analysis would cost US$557,838 per month.
- The potential savings was US$270,000 per month, or 32 percent savings.

The call distribution is shown below. As can be seen, the average busy hour (ABH) is 11:00 AM to noon and is 11 percent of the traffic.

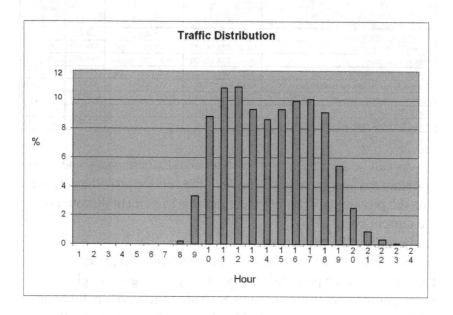

The study encompassed two different aspects:

- Negotiation of contracts and discounts
- Redesign of the network structure, including the deployment of a private network

Negotiations

This aspect consisted of comparing the company's current costs with the market alternatives available. The current telephone bill (toll-free) was calculated, verifying how much it would cost if it were charged using eight different charging plans from four service providers: Telemar (basic plan and thirty-one empresarial plan), Telefónica de España (basic plan), Intelig (two specific proposals), and Embratel (basic plan and one specific proposal). This calculation demanded the use of interconnection cost calculators. Doing them manually or even using Excel spreadsheets is virtually impossible. These simulations showed the correlation between the amount currently paid and the savings achievable through negotiation.

Charging plan	Value	Difference	%	Average price per minute
Telefonica de Spana Basic Plan	USD 2.234.624,00	USD 1.406.252,04	169,76%	USD 0,49
EMBRATEL basic plan	USD 2.078.482,77	USD 1.250.110,81	150,91%	USD 0,46
Telemar Basic plan	USD 2.054.728,00	USD 1.226.356,04	148,04%	USD 0,45
Telemar 31 Empresarial (RJ) plan	USD 1.064.075,22	USD 235.703,26	28,45%	USD 0,24
Telemar specific plan currently used	**USD 828.371,96**	USD 0,00	0,00%	USD 0,18
EMBRATEL specific proposal	USD 673.642,35	(USD 154.729,61)	-18,68%	USD 0,15
Intelig (1) specific proposal	USD 752.195,65	(USD 76.176,31)	-9,20%	USD 0,17
Intelig (2) specific proposal	USD 687.619,40	(USD 140.752,56)	-16,99%	USD 0,15

As can be seen in the spreadsheet above, there was some room to obtain savings by negotiating with the service providers. There was the possibility of achieving at least a 15 percent discount off the current costs.

Redesigning the Structure

Although there was room to obtain discounts through negotiations, there was also the possibility of achieving savings through redesigning the network. Design analysis comes both before and after quotes and may be part of final negotiations to ensure the cost structure contracted fits the new design optimally. With this objective, the traffic was mapped. The telephone bill was analyzed, identifying the origination and destination of traffic (traffic matrix) and verifying several network alternatives, including the alternative of building a private network.

The optimized structure identified included twenty-two regional nodes (as shown below) connected to Rio de Janeiro through dedicated circuits, where local numbers were adopted in each one of these twenty-two nodes. The toll-free number would work only outside these twenty-two areas. This structure cost US$557,838 per month, generating a saving of 32 percent (US$270,000) off the current expenditure.

The study also considered the cost of building these nodes (considering the TCO), including the hardware lease cost and real estate rental costs. The twenty-two nodes were as shown below:

	Node Name	Area code	Total number of users associated to the node	Number of users local	Number of users between 50 and 100Km	Number of users between 101 and 300Km	Number of users between 301 and 700Km	Number of users above 700Km
1	BELO HORIZONTE	312	109.203	47.843		15.821	32.126	
2	JUIZ DE FORA	322	38.946	17.501		10.783	10.662	
3	UBERLANDIA	342	59.831	15.509		9.408	29.371	
4	MACEIO	822	52.363	20.072		2.699	29.266	
5	MANAUS	922	28.854	21.888		182	312	
6	FEIRA DE SANTANA	752	51.236	26.508	3.708	2.822	4.363	
7	ITABUNA	732	33.819	18.516		646	9.574	
8	SALVADOR	712	35.485	34.379		1.106		
9	FORTALEZA	852	86.730	66.795		1.174	7.682	
10	BRASILIA	612	108.283	69.901	18.785	2.849	2.666	
11	VITORIA	272	78.184	38.052		3.990	33.158	
12	GOIANIA	622	82.807	62.717		5.889	12.435	
13	SAO LUIS	982	30.017	14.532		2.339	4.147	
14	CUIABA	653	46.450	23.131		92	3.032	
15	BELEM	912	22.597	18.396	288	334	146	0
16	JOAO PESSOA	832	36.580	24.787		4.658	7.063	0
17	RECIFE	812	102.397	90.704	3.236		8.457	
18	CURITIBA	412	96.423	38.524		7.783	23.711	0
19	RIO DE JANEIRO	21	113.873	85.752	7.465	1.172	19.484	138.635
20	NATAL	842	26.537	25.189			1.348	
21	PORTO ALEGRE	512	52.124	27.666	225	3.571	15.714	0
22	SAO PAULO	11	106.302	60.125		23.184	22.993	
	TOTAL		1.399.041	848.487	33.707	100.502	277.710	138.635
	Percentage		100.00%	60.85%	2.41%	7.18%	19.85%	9.91%

The topology implemented was a star configuration, although some marginal gains could be obtained through composing flows over the same physical paths, for example, traffic from Porto Alegre and Curitiba coming to Rio de Janeiro through São Paulo.

Through the deployment of tools, it also becomes possible to execute simulations identifying how much the structure would cost if we distributed IVRs and if the local callers paid for the calls.

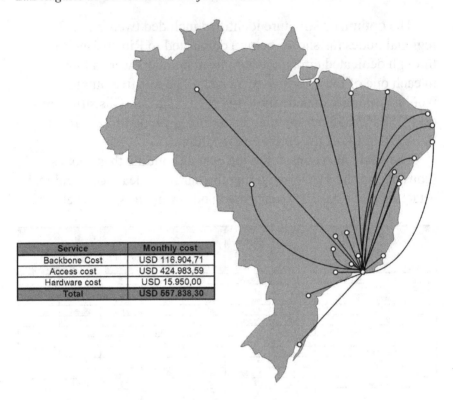

Service	Monthly cost
Backbone Cost	USD 116.904,71
Access cost	USD 424.983,59
Hardware cost	USD 15.950,00
Total	USD 557.838,30

As can be seen, this kind of analysis not only generated substantial economies, but also made possible the evaluation of several operational scenarios.

As can be seen through this case, the savings achievable through traditional negotiation (15 percent) are far below what could be achieved by rearranging the structure. An interesting aspect of this case in particular was the fact that the organization did not implement the cheapest capitation structure. The current provider was contacted and presented with the study. The company explained that, if a substantial discount was not provided, it would implement the project. Confronted with the alternative of losing everything, the telco gave up and offered a discount that brought the monthly value close to $560,000. The company threatened not only to build a capitation network, but also to let the access cost be paid by the user, a situation where Telemar would lose almost 60 percent of the access fees.

This case gives us a classical example of how well-conducted planning can help to extract discounts from the telco. As we saw, using a traditional kick-the-telco approach, we would not go much beyond 15 percent.

13.4 Telcos (Integrated Solutions Providers) and Complete Outsourcing Providers

Telcos may need these techniques when facing two distinct situations:

- When preparing proposals for enterprises where part of the client's sites are located outside its own area of coverage
- When expanding its own infrastructure

These two situations will be presented in the cases in this section. When a service provider is preparing proposals for enterprises whose points of presence are distributed beyond its own coverage area, it becomes important for the service provider to identify the optimum structure possible. The service provider has to minimize the cost of transporting the client's traffic through the uncovered area in order to prepare an attractive proposal and maximize its own profitability. The need for the techniques described in this book will grow as the percentage of the client's points of presence not covered by the service provider's own network grows.

In these cases, the only way to produce a competitive proposal is studying the traffic flows carefully and then arranging them in such way as to take advantage of cheap interconnection possibilities as much as possible. It is exactly what the techniques described in this book allows us to do.

When expanding its own infrastructure, the telco uses the same techniques but now the emphasis is changed. There is no separate customer with requirements to meet. The telco is its own customer. The techniques described in this book make it possible to establish the optimal correlation between geographical dispersion of the users, traffic volumes, and flows and interconnection costs involved when building a WAN, indicating exactly how the ideal structure would be to support a given traffic originated by a given population. This is exactly the kind of analysis needed when planning a telco expansion. Expansion in this context can mean increasing the coverage or adding new services.

13.4.1 Carrier Prepares a Proposal for a Worldwide Enterprise

This case describes a process developed within a Canadian carrier whose network covers approximately one hundred POPs throughout Canada and key cities in the United States. The client for whom the proposal was prepared was an American-based company with a worldwide presence. It had six hundred and ninety branches across the world, including nineteen branches in Canada and two hundred and eighty in the United States.

What Triggered the Process

The Canadian carrier was preparing a proposal to outsource the voice services of an American-based corporation with worldwide presence. The Canadian carrier had a complicated problem; that is, how to provide an attractive proposal given that they owned the infrastructure only inside Canada and in a small area in the United States. In addition, the international carriers, whose services the Canadian carrier relied on to connect the client's international locations, were themselves preparing proposals.

To make things worse, the client had less than 5 percent of its sites inside the area that the Canadian carrier covered directly. Faced with the fact that it was contracting the international links from companies which were themselves concurrent, the Canadian carrier had to somehow guarantee the optimization of the needed flows. It became clear that the only way to produce a competitive proposal would be to study the traffic flows carefully and then arrange them in such way as to take advantage of cheap interconnection possibilities as much as possible.

The only way to identify the optimal solution in such a problem would be deploying design tools and, through them, selecting the best arrangement. In this particular case, the ideal arrangement was identified by deploying two major international carriers to provide the main international links and nine regional ones to provide the regional interconnections. This arrangement was identified among virtually millions of possibilities.

The Strategy Adopted

The strategy adopted was very classical in many aspects:

- We identified the all the company's sites and volumes. The client made this task easier by providing a very detailed traffic matrix.
- We identified all the prices and interconnection availabilities of all eleven carriers, international and regional.
- We identified all possible topological arrangements, identifying all possible topological scenarios. (Understanding scenario as the number of sites that make a node feasible).
- We identified the flow's arrangements that would provide the most cost-effective solution.

All these steps were taken using exactly the same techniques described in this book.

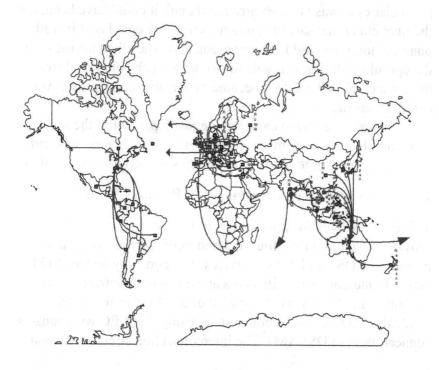

Results Achieved

The tools were able to produce a network structure almost 10 percent cheaper than the cheapest proposal. This was a remarkable result considering most proponents had a much larger percentage of the client's sites covered by their own network. But the outcome was not completely positive because the client was not interested just in price. It also wanted to have the biggest possible percentage of its network supported by the outsourcer's own infrastructure.

Nevertheless, the Canadian carrier made the client's short list against all odds because it was able to select the most cost-effective solution by combining all possible topologies and routes with all possible service providers. An interesting aspect about this case is the fact that the client used the Canadian carrier proposal to press the other proponents by saying, "If a Canadian carrier with less than 5 percent of its own network supporting my sites and subcontracting all other 95 percent can give us this price, you surely can do better."

The ultimate beneficiary of the carefully crafted design in this particular case was not the carrier, although it could have been, but the final client that saw how much its network could cost if well planned (topology and flow arrangements). The client armed with the optimized design was able to extract a much better deal from the large carriers because it became aware how much the network could be costing.

This was an extreme case, having just 5 percent of the network supported by its own infrastructure. If one of the big carriers had tried this approach, it would have surely smashed the competition.

13.4.2 Service Provider Evaluates Its Business Model

This case involves an American data communication service provider with more than four hundred POPs across North America, providing HDSL and ADSL services. The company had an ATM network interconnecting its POPs and a complete infrastructure of routers and DSLAMs. Almost all of its POPs were located inside the ILEC's co-location system, using the ILEC wire pairs to connect users to DSLAMs. The interconnection circuits between nodes were provided by three carriers: MCI/WorldCom, AT&T, and Qwest.

What Triggered the Process

The service provider was unable to provide voice services. So, each time a new user decided to use its ADSL service, the company had to ask the local ILEC to provide a second pair. The existent one was used for the ILEC POT line. But the ILECs were not very anxious to provide this second pair because they had their own data services. Consequently, they usually postponed the request until they reached the limit imposed by law (FCC regulations). Meanwhile, the potential new client received a visit from the ILEC sales representative. In addition, research conducted by the service provider showed that most users wanted only one company providing both services (voice and data) and charging them together.

These facts were strongly hindering the company's ability to increase its market share. To make things worse, the service provider had to pay the equivalent of three months of its monthly charge just to cover the ILEC second pair installation fee. Consequently, if the service provider could provide voice access, it would improve installation speed, reduce costs, and be able to provide only one bill to clients. Furthermore, the company knew the peak data and voice traffic were not coincidental. So there was some room in its ATM network to transport voice.

The Strategy Adopted

At first, the company was not even considering transporting voice through its own ATM network. The main idea was to maximize the pairs and send the voice calls back to the ILEC in the node. After verifying that these costs would not be much lower than implementing the whole solution and seeing the revenue possibilities, they decided to address the whole issue (voice access and transport).

To solve the problem described, it created a model where the service provider could analyze the correlation between the percentage of potential clients using voice and the cost to provide voice service. The model showed the company had to have at least 2 percent of all clients in their points of presence (COs) to make the service feasible. This task was relatively difficult because the company's market share was, on average, exactly 2 percent.[16] So implementing the voice service would be feasible as long as the company could convince all its clients to switch its voice services from the local ILECs. If more than 2 percent of existing clients and all new users took both services, the cost curve would remain below the revenue curve, though it would oscillate in ranges of twenty-five thousand users. That means that, in each twenty-five thousand new users, they had a peak of profitability.

The fact that the company could not implement the infrastructure in parts created an additional difficulty. If it did, the network would be unable to take some of the calls. Consequently, most of the revenue would not be achievable, annulling the benefits of a gradual implementation.

Another interesting conclusion was that, although the company could maximize its existing ATM network if it added voice service, this infrastructure would be able to handle less than 10 percent of the additional traffic that users generated. So, if just 10 percent of its actual clients (ADSL) decided to use the voice service, the existing ATM network would be able to handle this additional traffic without an increase in the available bandwidth. This does not mean the configuration would be profitable. Even though the company would not need to increase bandwidth, they would still need to build an expensive voice apparatus (class five switches, SS7 integration, voice management, billing, and so forth).

Results Achieved

Using design tools allowed the calculation of these structures to be fast and opened the possibility to make many calculations using several traffic volumes. Through these analyses, it becomes possible to establish the correlation between volume and cost. The possibility to set many volume scenarios is extremely useful because it allows us to see how the infrastructure cost changes depending on the volume transported. So it made us able to simulate the business case and identify the ROI and break-even point of the project. In summary, we could build the service

---

16   This was a little bit more on the East Coast area, but less in the West and Central areas.

provider business model and, consequently, simulate all volume scenarios.

13.4.3 ISP Optimizes Its WAN

This case describes a WAN optimization project conducted in one of the largest Brazilian ISPs. The company was the result of a merger between six service providers. Besides providing Internet access, it also provided data center outsourcing and Web hosting. The company had two hundred employees distributed into its four main offices. The company provided Internet access to more than two hundred and ninety large organizations in Brazil, and it was looking for opportunities to reduce its operational costs. The analysis covered three aspects of the WAN:

- **Circuit's real utilization verification:** This analysis shows that, if the nominal bandwidths of the circuits are really necessary, it opens the possibility to get savings from reducing them. Check if the contracted circuits are underused by using analytical tools called *curve readers*.
- **Topology verification:** This analysis using an analytical design tool allows the identification if there are opportunities of cost savings through rearranging the network structure.
- **Prices verification:** This identifies if there are possible gains attainable from renegotiating the values currently paid and shows, within which limits such gains stand. In this specific case, we compared the company's current prices with the costs of other companies of similar size. The study also included verification between the company's sites physical distribution and the available telcos' infrastructure. We used tools called *interconnection cost calculators*.

The basic data used to execute this study were:

- The list of the circuits (including all technical and administrative data about each one)
- The MRTG measurements (traffic measurements of each circuit)

- The contracts with the telcos (economical and contractual information)

The organization had two hundred and ninety circuits contracted with thirteen telcos as follows:

Service Provider	Number of circuits	Value in Brazilian Reais	Value in US dollars	% do gasto total
AESCON	8	R$ 16.756,86	USD 6.444,95	3,46%
AT&T	44	R$ 61.465,99	USD 23.640,77	12,71%
Brasil Telecom	5	R$ 2.999,00	USD 1.153,46	0,62%
D3	2	R$ 2.068,00	USD 795,38	0,43%
Diveo	1	R$ 1.294,00	USD 497,69	0,27%
Eletropaulo Telecom	2	R$ 4.504,00	USD 1.732,31	0,93%
Embratel	10	R$ 63.648,96	USD 24.480,37	13,16%
Global Crossing	1	R$ 34.847,75	USD 13.402,98	7,20%
Iqara	28	R$ 34.198,69	USD 13.153,34	7,07%
MetroRED	30	R$ 37.033,80	USD 14.243,77	7,66%
Telefonica	82	R$ 115.831,99	USD 44.550,77	23,95%
Telemar	76	R$ 108.241,12	USD 41.631,20	22,38%
Canbrás	1	R$ 781,00	USD 300,38	0,16%
Total	290	R$ 483.671,16	USD 186.027,37	100,00%

Bandwidth Usage Used vs. Contracted

The goal of this study is to verify if the contracted bandwidth corresponds to the traffic needed shown by the MRTG measurement tool. This analysis also allows the comparison between different technologies. Through this process, it becomes possible to compare alternatives such as using a packet network (using defined EIR and CIR values) or using dedicated clear channels.

It was identified that the network had an overcapacity of approximately 15 percent, and this volume could be reduced with correspondent economical gains without any damage to the network performance. However, the organization's management considered that its clients were not prepared to have their access bandwidth reduced, so this line of action was not pursued further.

Topological Analysis

The topological analysis aimed to adjust the current topology (four aggregation nodes) to the real physical distribution of the client's sites, trying to guarantee the minimum cost possible to the last mile circuits. It was verified if the current interconnection strategy is compatible with the traffic interest and, above all, if the geographical distribution of the aggregation nodes and telco POPs are compatible with the location of client's sites within the large cities (São Paulo and Rio de Janeiro where 90 percent of the sites are located). It was done in order to identify some negotiable advantage when dealing with the service providers. It basically matched the client's sites with the telco's infrastructure and current and potential aggregation nodes (with precision of meters).

This study identifies the clustering effect specific to the organization. This effect is demonstrated by the variation of the percentage of the sites located within distance ranges from a node when we vary the number and location of nodes. The distance ranges defined were:

Range 0	Range 1	Range 2	Range 3	Range 4	Range 5	Range 6	Range 7	Range 8
< 5 Km	5 Km <= X < 10 Km	10 Km <= X < 20 Km	50 Km <= X < 70 Km	70 Km <= X < 100 Km	100 Km <= X < 200 Km	100 Km <= X < 200 Km	200 Km <= X < 300 Km	>=300 Km

The topological study by itself is not enough to indicate the optimized WAN. It happens because a WAN's cost also depends on the interconnection costs, which are not always distance-sensitive. Nevertheless, this analysis gives us a good view of what tends to be the ideal topology. This study can also help when dealing with service providers because it demonstrates with great precision the site's physical distribution within the cities (region, avenue, and so forth), which can be a fundamental factor when negotiating discounts. The following spreadsheet gives a good view of the clustering effect of this specific organization:

Ranges	Range 0	Range 1	Range 2	Range 3	Range 4	Range 5	Range 6	Range 7	Range 8
Number of nodes	< 5 Km	5 Km < X < 10 Km	10 Km < X < 20 Km	50 Km < X < 70 Km	70 Km < X < 100 Km	100 Km < X < 200 Km	100 Km < X < 200 Km	200 Km < X < 300 Km	> 300 Km
1	32,66%	21,74%	9,91%	0,72%	2,65%	7,55%	0,72%	0,00%	0,00%
2	44,65%	24,66%	15,89%	1,20%	2,65%	7,63%	2,17%	0,08%	0,00%
3	51,83%	24,66%	15,89%	3,65%	0,80%	0,48%	1,53%	0,08%	0,00%
4	53,76%	24,66%	15,89%	1,72%	0,80%	0,52%	1,49%	0,08%	0,00%
5	55,05%	24,66%	15,89%	1,72%	0,80%	0,52%	0,20%	0,52%	0,00%
6	55,69%	24,66%	15,89%	1,72%	0,24%	0,48%	0,16%	0,52%	0,00%
7	56,09%	24,66%	15,89%	1,72%	0,24%	0,48%	0,16%	0,52%	0,00%
8	56,49%	24,66%	15,89%	1,72%	0,24%	0,08%	0,16%	0,52%	0,00%
9	56,77%	24,66%	15,89%	1,72%	0,24%	0,08%	0,24%	0,16%	0,00%
12	57,33%	24,66%	15,97%	1,24%	0,08%	0,08%	0,24%	0,16%	0,00%
14	57,65%	24,66%	15,97%	1,24%	0,08%	0,08%	0,24%	0,00%	0,00%
16	57,85%	24,66%	15,97%	1,12%	0,16%	0,00%	0,16%	0,00%	0,00%
22	58,33%	24,66%	15,97%	0,96%	0,08%	0,00%	0,00%	0,00%	0,00%
60	100,00%	0,00%	0,00%	0,00%	0,00%	0,00%	0,00%	0,00%	0,00%

A careful matching was executed between the site's location and the public infrastructure available (telco by telco). Such analysis made it possible for the good discounts to be achieved. The organization knew exactly what each provider had near each site.

The following drawing shows an example of the company's sites (X) within a public infrastructure. In this drawing, the dark grey dots are the company's sites, and the grey and black lines are the telco's infrastructure. (In this case, Iqara, a British gas company.)

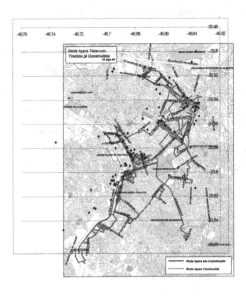

Results Achieved

Applying the strategies and tools described, the organization managed to get a direct monthly savings of 33 percent. These gains involved rearranging the circuits, canceling, and contracting. If we consider the migration costs (diluted throughout 36 months using a 1.27 percent p.m. financing rate), simultaneous operation, penalties, and installation fees, the monthly reduction was 25 percent over the current expenditures.

This effort generated R$120,000 (US$45,000) per month in savings. Although the percentage may not sound so impressive, we have to remember the fact that it was a very well-run infrastructure and the internal team had already done almost everything they could in order to reduce the operational costs. The tools here were used as a last resort to try to ditch additional savings.

13.5 Hardware Vendors

Hardware vendors are an important group of potential users of these techniques. They can be enormously impacted by them. Analyzing the network's structure is the best way to make the case for network rearrangements and hardware renovations. In addition, the savings identified usually surpass many times any necessary investment in hardware.

13.6 Situations Offering Unique Opportunities for Redesign

There are some situations where the techniques described here can be particularly useful. We are describing such situations and giving a real-life case about how the techniques were deployed and how they helped the organizations involved. The two special consideration situations are:

- When two organizations are merging
- When an organization is deciding to outsource its telecommunications infrastructure

When two organizations merge their operations, telecommunications operational cost is undoubtedly one source from where savings are expected. In these situations, the strongest

IT/telecommunications side of the merger traditionally takes over the process and usually regroups the new sites around its own. This strategy usually generates quick migrations and some savings.

The traditional approach does not take full advantage of the savings achievable by really analyzing the new structure, including both organizations' POPs. This moment (merger) is the perfect opportunity to reevaluate the telecommunications network. Aggregation nodes, which were not feasible with only one organization's traffic, may become feasible now. Actual nodes may overlap each other, and new patterns of traffic may appear in both organizations, given interchange of applications. All these changes demand a more detailed reevaluation than the already overloaded IT teams are usually able to perform.

13.6.1 Merger of Two WANs

Company X was a Brazilian bank based in São Paulo with one hundred branches and forty-five hundred employees, which had just bought Company Y, another Brazilian bank based in Belo Horizonte with one hundred and four branches and thirty-five hundred employees. Company X expended US$1.395 million monthly on telecommunications while Company Y expended US$554,301 monthly.

The Strategy Adopted

Company X wanted to integrate both networks as soon as possible. The geographical distributions of both organizations overlapped in some areas, but they were complementary in others. It was perceived that big savings could be achieved by merging both structures. But the strategy for the merger was not very clear. The opinions inside Company X were divided between those who advocated a more traditional approach (disconnect Company Y's sites from its nodes and connect them to Company X's nodes) and those who wanted to use this opportunity to rearrange the whole structure.

Finally, after some internal debate, the idea of using the opportunity to improve the whole structure won, and the decision to do the analysis was made. The main argument against recalculating the whole structure was the fact that it would create unnecessary delays. This was the opinion of some of Company X's people. Besides, it was not clear at that point if the difference between a more traditional approach and a complete rearrangement would be large enough to compensate for the foreseen delays. A very common misperception is that this kind of analysis is too time-consuming.

The analysis was performed using design tools and conducted as if both organizations were only one. The new topology of this new combined structure was identified. Having the ideal configuration, it became possible to identify all that needed to be rearranged to adjust the previous structures to a new unified one. In this case, the analysis considered the interconnection alternatives among two nationwide IXCs and three RBOCs, a relatively complex case. The service providers' alternative carriers included:

Nationwide IXCs	EMBRATEL
	COMSAT
RBOCs	TELEMAR
	TELEFONICA
	BRASIL TELECOM

As can be seen in the following spreadsheet, the ideal structure was identified as having eleven nodes with 85 percent of all sites located within less than two hundred kilometers from some node (distance range 3 "Degrau" and below).

City	QUANT	Range 0	Range 1	Range 2	Range 3	Range 4	Range 5	Range 6	Range 7	Range 8
Brasília	20	5	0	0	5	0	0	0	2	8
Belo Horizonte	34	22	0	2	3	1	2	0	2	2
Juiz de Fora	12	4	0	2	1	3	2	0	0	0
Londrina	10	2	0	1	3	0	4	0	0	0
Florianópolis	15	2	0	2	2	2	6	1	0	0
São Paulo	55	51	0	4	0	0	0	0	0	0
Ribeirão Preto	18	3	0	3	8	4	0	0	0	0
Campinas	13	5	0	6	2	0	0	0	0	0
Rio de Janeiro	27	25	2	0	0	0	0	0	0	0
TOTAL	204	119	2	20	24	10	14	1	4	10

Results Achieved

The results were impressive. The possibility to reduce 65 percent of the current telecommunications costs was identified. Although important, the reduction of monthly costs was not the only benefit. The bandwidth availability was doubled, and the network resilience was improved through deployment of backups.

In addition, some collateral benefits, such as hardware nodes standardization and a completely new network management center, were implemented.

Despite the concerns about delays, the whole analysis took just one month, which was much less than initially estimated, and constituted an enormous improvement over the initial estimated savings. Following the traditional approach, the savings expectations were of 20 percent. The analysis identified 65 percent. In fact, this was a classic case where the automated design process proved itself over more traditional strategies.

As already discussed in chapter seven, a company trying to decide between purchasing equipment instead of relying on a service provider must consider a combination of factors. The obvious comparison is between up-front capital and ongoing maintenance costs associated with purchasing equipment instead of leasing similar functions from a service provider. Then there are more intangible issues related to things like control and level of responsiveness.

The decision to outsource a network or not is often hindered by the fact that most outsource evaluations are based on the actual company's expenditures compared with the foreseen outsource price. As described in chapter seven, in most cases, the company could be doing a much better job in-house than it is actually doing. So the described comparison is not fair. It often makes outsourcing look like a much better alternative than it actually is.

So, in order to rationalize as much as possible the decision of whether to outsource a network or not, it is absolutely crucial that the in-house cost-optimized structure is identified. Then use this value to evaluate outsource alternatives. Following this strategy, you can guarantee a fair comparison between an in- and outsourced solution and make a fair comparison between the intangible factors and right quantitative figure.

13.6.2 Organization Analyzes Outsourcing Alternatives

The company is a worldwide travel and financial services company. It employs around three thousand Canadians in one hundred and twenty-seven branches. It is also a leading provider of travel-related services in Canada and assists companies in managing and controlling their business and travel expenses.

Situation

The organization's network was outsourced three years ago. A series of problems related to the network reliability, performance, and cost convinced management to reevaluate the situation. The first step was to identify the causes of the network's underperformance. The second step was to identify the solution and calculate how much it would cost. The company wanted to know how much the new network would cost, including installation and operation (using internal and external personnel). This information would allow them to decide whether to keep the infrastructure outsourced or not. In addition, they wanted to determine a reasonable premium to pay the outsourcer if they decided to keep things as they are.

Analysis

The analysis showed that the ideal topological structure would have eight nodes with 90 percent of the one hundred and twenty-seven branches located less than two hundred kilometers from them.

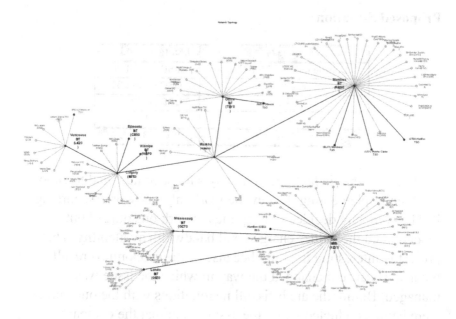

When analyzing the traffic and interconnection costs available and assuming a complete hardware renovation, the analytical software used identified a possible network monthly savings of US$107,659. This was almost half of the price that the outsourcer currently charged for the existing network. Besides being less expensive, the proposed structure was much more resilient (having backup for all main nodes) and had almost two times the bandwidth availability. So was identified the possibility of paying almost half the current cost to have a much better structure. By analyzing the alternatives, the tool found that, through topological rearrangement and voice integration, it would be possible to reduce costs from US$240,795 to US$133,135.

Current Situation

Service type	Monthly cost US$
Outside network PSTN calls	USD 151.555,79
Hardware	USD 20.000,00
Data circuits	USD 69.240,00
Total	USD 240.795,79

Proposed Situation

Service type	Monthly cost US$
Outside network PSTN calls	USD 73.374,00
Hardware	USD 11.521,86
Backbone	USD 28.000,00
Access	USD 20.240,00
Total	USD 133.135,86

Faced with this fact, the company's management had to choose between implementing the new network internally or outsourcing it. The company decided to keep the network outsourced but renegotiated the values charged and bandwidth availability. This project is interesting not only because of the economical results, but also because it changed the way in which the issue was managed. Before the analysis, all negotiations with the outsourcer were being conducted under the assumption that the company would pay more for a network with more bandwidth and resilience.

The outsourcer response was, "If you want more bandwidth and resilience, it is going to cost you more." The study broke this paradigm by showing that the company could have a better structure for less money. In addition, the decision to outsource or not was placed in a completely different perspective. It became clear that, within a certain price range, outsourcing would be a valid alternative. The company said, "We agree to outsource as long as your price is equal to or slightly bigger than the cost of implementing and operating the network ourselves."

Results Achieved

Because of this process, the negotiation with the outsourcer was not based on the current price, but on the price that the company would be paying if it implemented the optimized network themselves. The negotiation determined the premium that the outsourcer would charge on top of this price to implement and manage the infrastructure, which was a quite different approach from the previous one. Because of the negotiation, the outsourcer agreed to charge a premium of just 10 percent over the calculated price.

14

Gathering the Data to Execute a WAN Analysis

In order to analyze the WAN, you need information. The accuracy and availability of data is crucial to this phase of planning a WAN. Failure to perform this phase correctly will jeopardize the whole analysis. This chapter describes which data are necessary to perform a WAN analysis and how this data can be gathered. If your intention is just to get a brief understanding of what information is necessary to perform the analysis, we would suggest that you skip some of the topics. When preparing this chapter, we had a difficult choice between being specific enough to allow more technical people to use this chapter as a manual reference and, at the same time, still keep it readable for the management. We hope to have succeeded in achieving both objectives.

The analysis required to implement a new WAN is a complex process that looks at information elements of the organization as well as service providers. In the event that the network has a significant global scope, it will dramatically increase the complexity of the process. The analysis process includes modeling of different possible solutions (heuristic problem). It also considers political realities and strategic decisions of the organization. This modeling function will highlight costs associated with organizational-driven decisions.

Gathering the information required to design a WAN is a difficult and intensive task. Companies usually do not have all the information necessary. Even when they have it, it is frequently spread across many departments without any consolidation. "99 percent perspiration, 1 percent inspiration" is a good description for the process of planning a WAN. The data gathering is undoubtedly the perspiration part. It is tedious and difficult, but a key part of enabling a cost-effective and operationally sound WAN environment.

Some of the information required for the analysis is under control of service providers, and there is no correlation between charges in different countries, even when using the same service provider. Additionally, obtaining, for example, interconnection costs from service providers is not always an easy task. Dealing with consulting companies to get at this information poses a risk as well. These companies often use institutional knowledge based on outdated tariff structures.

For a telecommunications manager whose job consists of planning a WAN only one time, there are specialized companies, which sell information regards tariffs and hardware costs in specific areas.

Consulting companies usually buy the information when planning a WAN for the first time within a given area. If you are a telecommunication manager of a large organization consider doing the same; although you may not have a recurring need for this information, it is fundamental to this process. The information necessary to perform the analysis can be divided into three groups:

- **The information exclusively related to the infrastructure analyzed:** The population to be served by the network, POPs, number of sources/destinations of traffic, traffic patterns, server locations, and existing infrastructure and current contracts
- **The information related to the environment where the infrastructure is deployed:** The interconnection costs, hardware costs, interconnection possibilities, costs of personnel, and tariff system
- **The nonexclusive information:** Typical traffic pattern for given kinds of applications, typical interconnection costs, and everything that can be deployed as valid inference/ generalization in the absence of specific data

Typically, the team performing this analysis should follow the described sequence:

- Verify with the organization and environmental data sources (PTT, carriers, and vendors) in order to identify which data are available.
- After verifying what is missing, consider the effort involved to get the data and compare it with the nonexclusive information available.
- Engage the project sponsor. Discuss and identify which data would be worthy of researching/measuring and which ones would be acceptable to be achieved through inference based on nonexclusive information. Evaluate the trade-off between the effort and cost involved to get the exact information and lack of precision due to using nonexclusive information and the risk this poses to the project.

Factors such as time availability, how well organized the organization is (IT maturity), and political and conflicting agendas of the different departments are decisive or often a major driver when deciding what to do. For instance, if we have a very strict deadline, we would be more prone to rely on nonexclusive information (generalizations) than doing precise measurements. On the other hand, if we have a very politically conflicting internal environment, we would be pushed to rely on accurate data rather than doing any inference and relying on institutional information, as these will often provide different answers depending on which IT/user group you interview.

Sometimes evaluating how well organized a company is makes us decide whether to go ahead using measurements or perform inferences. It is hard to draw a line in this matter, but, whatever strategy you follow, be sure to double-check your data. The worse possible scenario is be caught by a wrong conclusion due to poorly verified information based on nonexclusive data.

14.1 Organization's Specific Information

As when planning a logistic network, when designing a telecommunications network, it is crucial to understand traffic flows in all their details. The specific information necessary to plan a WAN can be grouped as follows: traffic sources (origins and destinations), types of loads to be transported, and traffic volume, profiles, and interests. Note that all traffic information can be grouped by type of application (voice, data, and images). Traffic flow profiles and volume over time are also parts of these analyses.

If there is a WAN in place, which is usually the case, we also have to identify hardware already in use (including capacity and cost) and miscellaneous information (including contracts, circuits, and topology among others). These are what we call *primary information*. They have to be identified in order to make the planning of the network possible. All other analyses are generated based on this information combined with the environmental ones.

14.1.1 Traffic Sources (Origins and Destinations)

As in any other logistic network, we need to understand the origin and destination of the traffic to be transported. Depending on which kind of WAN we are planning, this identification can be very complex.

When designing a WAN, the number of people, workstations, and servers must be known. These are our primary traffic sources, although which is important may differ for different applications. For example, if we are designing a mobile phone network, each user will be our source/destination of traffic. As already mentioned in chapter three, we refer to the sources/destinations of traffic as *traffic generator units*.

Consequently, to design a WAN, in theory, it is necessary to identify the location of all traffic generator units. This level of granularity, however, is not ideal, not only because it adds too much effort to the calculations, but also because this effort does not add any significant benefit to the design process. We can usually group the traffic generator units and treat them grouped without jeopardizing the quality of the design. In this book, we will refer to the group of traffic generator units as *traffic units*. When defining the traffic units, we can adopt several strategies, as demonstrated by the following examples:

- We may not be able to guarantee exactly from where each user of a bank's call center will originate its call, but we can assume as a simplifying premise with a high degree of certainty that the majority of the users will originate their calls from the same area code of their branches. So we may group the users by their branch area codes.

- When analyzing a mobile network, we do not know with complete certainty from where each user will originate each call. However, based on factors such as the addresses of the users, population density, number of economically active individuals per area, and typical commute, we may be able to build a reasonable model though which we can group the users within the city.

- When designing a corporate WAN, identifying the origins and destinations of the traffic is usually very direct, for example, an organization's branches. Even then, we must be attentive to aspects such as remote workers and call center users, whose locations are not so easily identifiable. It is usually possible to group the users by site.

Regardless of the difficulties involved when mapping the origin and destination of traffic, we can usually establish a reasonable logic that brings us close to the reality. It is crucial that we manage to identify all traffic units (encompassing all traffic generator units) and associate them geographically (associating with specific geodesic coordinates to allow calculations). In this context of a corporative network, the term *site* usually corresponds to our definition of traffic units. The reader must be aware that, depending on the type of the design (public network, call center, and so forth), the term *traffic units* may have different meanings (area code, geographical region, and so forth).

Conceptually, we are establishing the lines and columns of the traffic matrix of the network. Theoretically, we could have a situation where all sites or traffic generator units speak among themselves. However, in practical terms, corporate WANs are used to having their data traffic pattern well defined between the workstations and the organization's servers.

In the case of voice, the traffic interest tends to be more disperse, either the internal traffic (intraorganization) or external traffic (extraorganization). In this case, we usually build two different sets of traffic matrixes. First is the intraorganization matrix where the lines and columns are the organization's sites. Second is the extraorganization traffic. In this case, the lines and columns are the area codes. The data and voice flows among the sources and destinations (the content of our traffic matrixes) are defined based on a given period, for example, per hour, per day, or per month.

14.1.2 Types of Loads to Be Transported

The type of load to be transported is a fundamental piece of information required to analyze a WAN. Typically, the ITU-T classifies the possible services to be provided by a network in four types:

- **Conversational services:** Services provided end-to-end in real time such as video telephony, telephony, and telecommand
- **Recovered services:** Provide possibility to recover information remotely stored, such as videotext and video-on-demand
- **Message services:** Provide communication between users through data storage units with functions of store and forward (e-mail, voice mail, and data transmission)
- **Distribution services:** Includes audio and video distribution, stock quotations, and so forth
  The patterns of the traffic generated by each one of the services are very different. We divide them into three classes:
- **Ping-pong transactions (burst):** Use variable bandwidth intermittently
- **Bulk data (transfer continuous with variable rate):** Use variable bandwidth continually
- **Voice traffic (continuous with constant rate):** Use a defined bandwidth continually

Each one of these services has different transport requirements. In general, we can organize them as defined by RFC 4594:

Service Class Name	Traffic Characteristics	Tolerance to		
		Loss	Delay	Jitter
Network Control	Variable size packets, mostly inelastic short messages, but traffic can also burst (BGP)	Low	Low	Yes
Telephony	Fixed-size small packets, constant emission rate, inelastic and low-rate flows	Very Low	Very Low	Very Low
Signaling	Variable size packets, somewhat bursty short-lived flows	Low	Low	Yes
Multimedia Conferencing	Variable size packets, constant transmit interval, rate adaptive, reacts to loss	Low-Medium	Very Low	Low
Real-Time Interactive	RTP/UDP streams, inelastic, mostly variable rate	Low-Medium	Very Low	Low
Multimedia Streaming	Variable size packets elastic with variable rate	Low-Medium	Medium	Yes
Broadcast Video	Constant and variable rate, inelastic, non-bursty flows	Very Low	Medium	Low
Low-Latency Data	Variable rate, bursty short-lived elastic flows	Low	Low-Medium	Yes
OAM	Variable size packets, elastic & inelastic flows	Low-Medium	Medium	Yes
High-Throughput Data	Variable rate, bursty long-lived elastic flows	Low	Medium-high	Yes
Standard	A bit of everything	Not specif	Not specif	Not specif
Low-Priority Data	Non-real-time and elastic	High	High	yes

14.1.3 Traffic Volume, Interest, and Profile

When defining the traffic volume of each service, we must first understand the following concept: We are trying to give a defined value (contracted bandwidth) to something, which is essentially dynamic, that is, has different values over time. So the calculations will result in a defined bandwidth value based on the traffic flow (data or voice flow) over time, trying to guarantee the minimum quality requirement during the peak times. The calculation is based on the applications deployed and the traffic profile. So, for each traffic unit (group of traffic generator units that are usually the organization's sites), we have to identify a discrete volume (defined bandwidth value to support the traffic) and a dynamic volume (traffic volume along the time).

Here it is important to understand that the discrete volume is just the defined value of a bandwidth that will support the dynamic traffic volume, guaranteeing a minimum level of service even during the peak moments. In this section, we are going to discuss how the information regarding the dynamic volume is obtained. Subsequently, we are going to demonstrate how, based on this information, we calculated the discrete volume (necessary defined bandwidth).

The first step is to identify the applications in use. Applications in this context can be voice, data, or image. With the applications identified, we must identify the traffic matrix. In case of data application, it would be where the locations of the workstations and servers running each application are.

The services that the network support are the key factors when designing a WAN. Their requirements in terms of quality define the necessary availability of throughput (discrete volume). Such quality requirements may involve using different parameters when calculating the necessary bandwidths. As a result, we have to typify each application and define the parameters that allow us to calculate the amount of traffic generated to be transported (dynamic and discrete). Some of these parameters should be measured; others are defined based on our perception of what is the acceptable QoS.

We recommend you minimize the application classification so as not to make it too granular. The ideal strategy is to group them by similar traffic profiles. This strategy simplifies the calculation processes without jeopardizing the results. A typical project would involve the following services:

Data

Corporative applications

E-mails

Web access

Voice

Corporative

Call-centers

We could expand each one of these services into subservices, but the gains would be marginal and likely not worth the additional effort. Of course, it is not a rule written in stone. In exceptional cases, we can and even should break down the traffic, for example, a specific application is the reason for the existence of the network. Nevertheless, generally, we should treat the traffic in a grouped manner.

We must be able to calculate the volumes in/out of the traffic units based on the number of traffic generator units located in each one. traffic generator units in this context can be workstations, people, and so forth. Based on this volume, we identify the necessary bandwidth. Establishing this correlation is crucial to allow us to simulate different scenarios.

To execute this calculation, we need to identify the traffic pattern (traffic pattern of a defined type of traffic) of a typical traffic generator unit. This pattern will be identified for all applications (or group of applications) on the network.

14.1.3.1 Data Traffic

To be able to identify the traffic pattern (discrete and dynamic) per traffic generator unit for each type of application, we need to execute measurements of a representative number of the links in use. This decision about what constitutes a representative sample depends on the geographic distribution of the usage of the applications. This will typically vary greatly between, for example, a global industrial conglomerate and a large retail company. The industrial conglomerate will typically have business units, which are themselves potentially very large organizations, that do not share any data centers or applications with other business units of the corporation. Often, the only shared activities are, for example, finance consolidation or business intelligence (BI) executed at a corporate level. The measurement should be executed, allowing the separation of the volumes by application type (or grouped applications).

To enable us to identify the parameters to calculate the necessary bandwidth, we must classify the application by traffic pattern, select the sample of traffic units to be measured, and conduct the measurement for an adequate period of time.

If we are designing a completely new network, it is not possible to execute measurements to identify the network traffic. In this situation, we should identify the traffic by identifying the applications to be supported by the network. Through lab analysis, we should figure out the demand of traffic of each one. Alternatively, a strategy of using reference measurements of other organizations that use similar type of applications could be used.

It is also important to define the period of the measurement to guarantee the samples really reflect reality. In most cases, the partial measurement (a week or two weeks) is enough. Nevertheless, traffic variations in specific periods of the month or in specific months within the year (for example, year-end processing) may affect the results. We must be attentive to such variations.

Once we execute the measurement, we separate the measurement logs by type of traffic (volume bits/sec) by period of time and generate the traffic curve. The result of the measurement will be a graphic by type of traffic, as demonstrated by the picture bellow.

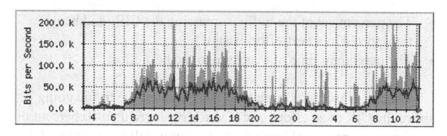

As we can see, the graphic shows the volumes along the time (dynamic volume). In this specific case, we have a measurement of a ping-pong traffic application of a traffic unit with five traffic generator units measured for a day. Based on the measured traffic, we obtain several parameters that will allow us to calculate the traffic pattern (discrete and dynamic) of the traffic generator units by type of traffic. Based on this pattern and number of traffic generator units located in each traffic unit (site), we calculate the necessary bandwidth for each site. In addition, based on the dynamic volume of the traffic measured, the traffic pattern of each traffic generator unit by type of traffic, and the number of traffic generator units located in each traffic unit (site), we can identify the traffic curve of each traffic unit (site).

The clear visualization of the traffic curve, as shown before, makes us able to understand the limits of the discrete volume (bandwidth actually contracted). Seeing how the traffic flows over time, we can see the percentage of the bandwidth in use at each moment. Such a view allows us to understand how the level of service varies along the day and, most importantly, during the peak hour.

The clear visualization of the traffic flow (dynamic) allows us to identify the percentage of the traffic that flows under and above the CIR (discrete volume), and allows us to see the maximum time of exposure to the best-effort type of services. Through this graphic, we understand the network performance as the users perceive it during the day. It enables us to analyze the tradeoff between bandwidth operating empty versus QoS during peak hours.

Here we have two parameters to work with:

- The percentage of the traffic surpassing the CIR (and being transported in a best-effort basis)
- The maximum time of exposure to the best effort

Usually, if we have more than 20 percent of the traffic going above the CIR (best effort) and if you have more than 10 percent of the time of exposure of best effort, your user will be suffering. Of course, in a sense, the perception of what is acceptable varies. It is hard to draw a precise line on this. In any event, we need to have a view about how the volume varies over time.

Traffic measurements can be executed by several specialized tools, such as MRTG, NetFlow collector, and so forth. In summary, when designing a telecommunications network, we must understand the services supported by it, identify the applications, identify their type, and identify a specific traffic pattern by traffic generator unit (dynamic and discrete).

Another aspect is the fact that, although we are calculating the traffic volume per type of application (grouped), such traffic flows will be combined through the connections. Once we have the traffic pattern (dynamic volume), we can calculate the discrete volume (bandwidth to be used by each traffic unit) easily.

Dynamic Volume Identification for Data Traffic

We identify the dynamic traffic pattern, dividing the measurement curves by the number of traffic generator units (workstations) of each measured traffic unit (site). In our example, that would be dividing the curve by five. Once we have this pattern, we multiply it by the number of traffic generator units (workstations) of each traffic unit where we want to know the curve. Then we sum the curves (if we have more than one type of traffic being measured) and get the totalized traffic curve of the traffic unit (site's curve).

Once we have the totalized traffic curve, using programs called *curve readers*, we calculate the area of the curve below a given CIR value. We do this calculation until the percentage of the area gets near to a given value (usually around 80 percent) or when the maximum time of best effort exposure gets below a given time (for example, ten seconds). This becomes the discrete volume (CIR value) to be used (contracted). The chosen value will support a given percentage of the traffic within the defined CIR, so it will not dispute bandwidth with others. What happens with traffic above the CIR that is transported with the quality is defined as *best effort*, meaning when bandwidth is available. The curve readers also help us to calculate the values of the EIR. We can repeat the process described to calculate the CIR, but now search for the EIR.

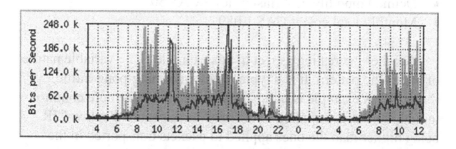

Here we have a bank branch with five workstations, using an application whose traffic is demonstrated by the graphic depicted in the picture shown before. The typical packet size is two hundred bytes (out) and one thousand bytes (in). Basically using a curve reader program, we manage to identify the total transported volume (per day) and value of CIR that guarantees that 80 percent of the traffic will be below it. Dividing this value by the number of workstation, we manage to get the pattern to define the CIR by traffic generator unit (workstation) and use this value to calculate the necessary bandwidth for all organization's sites based on the number of traffic generator units located in each site.

- CIR per workstation by application: 3,200 bits/s or 0.33 packets/s per workstation
- EIR per workstation by application: 8,192 bits/s or 1.17 packets/s per workstation
- Total transported volume: 13.2 million bits or 8,250 packets with 200 bytes per day per workstation

The percentage of traffic below the CIR is a parameter defined. We must define it based on our perception of what constitutes adequate QoS. Here we defined 80 percent. In this example, our service provider is charging a defined monthly value plus CA$0.001 per transported packet of 1,200 (below CIR) and CA$0.002 per packet transported above the CIR. So our monthly cost to this branch (if it had only this application) would be:

- (8,250 packets × 5 users × 21 days) × 0.80 × 0.001 = CA$ 693
- (8,250 packets ×5 users × 21 days) × 0.20 × 0.002 = CA$ 346
- Defined monthly cost (last mile) = CA$ 50
- Monthly total cost = CA$ 1,089

Another interesting aspect in this example is the variable nature of the traffic pattern. It is a typical pattern of ping-pong traffic (burst). This example is purely theoretical, and it is more common to find the charges applied to the packets transported below CIR being higher than the ones applied to packets transported in the best effort mode.[17]

17 The example above is for illustration purposes only and not based on any real scenario.

It is interesting to notice why it is necessary to have a clear view of both discrete and dynamic volume. In this particular example, the pricing strategy is based on the volume along the time (dynamic) and number of packets, not a defined volume (defined bandwidth).

Discrete Volume Definition Strategy for Data Traffic

The calculation of the discrete volume provides a defined bandwidth to support a given traffic flow based on measured parameters, if we are redesigning an existing network, and based on our perception of what is acceptable in terms of QoS. Each traffic pattern has its own formula through which we calculate the defined bandwidth. We are going to discuss some of them in the subsequent items. Here it is important to clarify that we are giving examples of how the math of the discrete volumes is done, although some variations/simplifications of these methods may be used also.

Ping-pong Transactions

Many different kinds of applications have a ping-pong traffic pattern. Basically, all transactions that depend on a request and an immediate answer can be classified as ping-pong. Examples of ping-pong applications are user sections traffic, internal Web pages, external Web pages, and client/server traffic. In estimating bandwidth requirements for ping-pong transactions using discrete definition strategy, there are several key variables:

- Think = User think-time (the amount of time a user needs between successive inquiries)
- K = The number of packets per transaction in both directions[18]
- M = Number of bytes per packet in any one direction
- Latency = Acceptable latency for this specific application
- Workstation = Number of workstations in the site

With this notation, the estimated bandwidth in any one direction is as follows: Data load (per application) = (8 ×

---

18 We are interested to know the amount of incoming traffic and outgoing traffic. From the branch point of view, we need to adopt the bigger one, but, if you look at it from an aggregation node point of view where you have more than one physical route, it can be different.

workstation × K × M)/((K × latency) + Think) bits/sec. All parameters must be identified during the busiest hour. Otherwise, our minimum QoS would not be achievable during the peak usage period.

Example of Discrete Volume Definition Strategy

As identified in the previous example, each user section sends an average of 150 packets of an average length of 200 bytes to the remote host and receives back an average of 300 packets of 1,000 bytes each hour (during the busiest hour). Following the formula: Data load (per application) = (8 × workstation × K × M)/((K × latency) +Think) bits/sec

Each user section sends an average of 150 packets of an average length of 200 bytes to the remote host and receives back an average of 300 packets of 1,000 bytes each hour (during the busiest hour). So the average user data load for this application would be: (300 × 1000) = 300,000 bytes per hour per user or 300,000 × 8 = 2.4 million bits/per hour per user. We may have to do the calculations in both directions if we are using some asymmetric technology: (K × latency) + think = one hour. This is because the known volume was within a one-hour measurement period. Considering that, the actual network latency is acceptable. Following: 2,400,000/3,600 seconds = 666,66 bits per second per user.

Now let's imagine we have one site with five computers/users so the traffic demand of 666,6 × 5 users = 3333,33 bits per second for this specific application. Adjusting for standard telco bandwidth, we would contract a permanent 14,400 bits/s circuit, which, considering our distance, would cost us CA$715.38.[19]

Bulk Data Transfers Transactions

Many different kinds of applications have a bulk data transfer traffic pattern. Basically, all transactions that depend on non-immediate data transfer can be classified as bulk data transfer transactions. Examples of bulk data transfer applications are connectionless data networks, internal e-mail traffic, external e-mail traffic, transfer/portioned data, replication, mirroring,

---

19   These are fictional values. The example above is for illustration purposes only and not based on any real scenario.

downloads, and uploads. When estimating bandwidth requirements for bulk data transfer transactions, there are several key variables:

- F = Size of the bulk data to be transferred
- O = Protocol overhead factor accounts for the TCP/IP and link layer overhead that each TCP segment must carry[20]
- R = transference time expectation in seconds

With this notation, the estimated bandwidth in any one direction is as follows: Data load (for each application) = Workstations × (F × O × 8 bits per byte)/R

Example of Discrete Volume Definition Strategy

Suppose a server in the United States sends 256 kilobytes chunks of data to a client in Europe. The client would like to see the data appear within five seconds, including all delays. The bandwidth needed would be:

(256 × 1.05 × 8)/5 seconds = 430 kilobits/second.

We should be careful setting the TCP/IP window size to at least 16 kilobytes (430 kilobits/sec × 0.3 seconds). Windows NT's default window size is 8 kilobytes. If the window size is smaller than 16 kilobytes for this connection, the required throughput will not be realized. Window sizes vary greatly with newer systems. The latest crop of Microsoft servers deals with dynamic windows in innovative ways. You need to be aware of the impact that TCP flow control will have on long latency connections. For bulk data transfer, WAN accelerators should be considered. This technology generally does three tasks, as follows: compression; caching of data streams (not files); and spoofing control flows for various applications, for example, control flows for Microsoft applications and TCP windowing mechanism.

The data that undergoes acceleration can be specified by source and/or destination ports. The technology is relatively new, but, despite its cost point, it could be very beneficial. Frequently, it is a must when dealing with certain types of traffic or high-

---

20 For a segment size of 1024 bytes, which is common, the protocol overhead factor is (1024 + 48)/1024 = 1.05 (approximately), or about 5 percent. End-user tolerance in a client/server application is usually between three and five seconds, including all delays.

speed global infrastructures with large latency characteristics. Deployment of acceleration devices is typical in environments that rely on global collaboration (follow-the-sun engineering) where fast transfer of bulk data is often a requirement. It is not our intent to build this technology into this model at this point. The important fact when using accelerators is what happens at a business level in terms of data movement through the network. If you plan to use accelerators, you will have to establish the math and build it into the design software.

14.1.3.2 Voice Traffic

It was generally common to have separate networks to transport voice and data. This was due to technical and historical reasons. However, this trend was reversed. Today, the general trend is to transport all kinds of traffic over the same infrastructure, where possible, because savings can usually be achieved by integrating voice and data over the same transport infrastructure and most technical problems that prevented us from performing this integration before were solved. This is mainly because IP has become the default protocol of transport.

In our analysis, when faced with the need to include voice as part of the services that the network provided, we treat it as an application. Of course, it is an application with a different set of requirements, but it is still just an application.

Typically, audio and video generate traffic continuously with constant rate with a high need for latency control. Voice and video are highly sensitive to transmission delays, although not to loss. We normally identify the voice volume based on the telephone bills and physical location of the people using the network. Today, in most cases, it is possible to get the bills in electronic format. Nevertheless, there are circumstances where the bills are not available. When it happens, we may use the billing system files or samples taken from chosen sites, as we do with the data traffic. Either way, using a complete verification or just a sample, our objective is to identify the traffic profile (pattern, interest, and volume) by traffic generator unit (user).

So the bills and geographical distribution of a given population is our starting point. For instance, when analyzing enterprise voice volume, the first information to be identified is telephone bills, the number of people per site, and their voice usage pattern.

We must use a bill whose month was representative of the organization's typical traffic. We may have organizations where there is a large traffic variance over the year. It depends on the type of service that the organization executed. A good strategy to overcome this problem is to use more than one month's sample, making the average or using the highest traffic month. It becomes particularly important when the difference between the month with the lower traffic and the month with the bigger traffic exceeds 15 percent. It is important to proceed in this way. Otherwise, our analysis will be distorted.

The subsequent explanations assume we had access to all of the organization's voice invoices. We will later detail the procedures when the invoices are not available.

Initially from the call logs, we extract the data for calls originating in the internal network and destined for mobile phones. We are dealing with the mobile-to-mobile traffic in a specific chapter. After the extraction, the remaining calls will be fixed-to-fixed calls. This data is then separated into two types of calls: intraorganization and extraorganization. To be able to execute this separation, we must identify all organization's trunks and all calls whose trunks of origin and destination belong to the organization. Once this separation is done, we use dedicated software to produce the traffic matrixes. Such matrixes are slightly different for intra- and extra-traffic:

- **Intraorganization:** Based on the intraorganization traffic, we generate the intraorganization traffic matrix, which has, as its columns and rows, the organization's traffic units (sites), indicating the volume in minutes; number of calls; and cost of the traffic among the organization's sites. Based on the number of traffic generator units (people) in each traffic unit (sites) and number of minutes (in/out), we identify the voice traffic pattern of the organization (internal). Here we have the traffic in and out.

- **Extraorganization:** Based on the extraorganization traffic logs, we generate the traffic matrix per area code, indicating the volume in minutes, number of calls, and cost of the traffic to provide the voice calls among the area codes. Based on the number of traffic generator units (people) in each traffic unit (sites) and number of minutes (out), we identify the voice traffic pattern of the organization (external). We have only the outbound traffic, although, based on the type of operation, we may be able to infer the inbound traffic.

When planning a telecommunications network, we must evaluate if the voice and data integration is economically attractive or not. Although it is often feasible to integrate voice and data, that does not mean it is always worth the added complexity. So we must be able to map the traffic and compare the cost of transporting it through a data network with the cost of transporting it in the traditional way through the public network. When doing this comparison, we should be able to compare not only the complete integration versus the transport of voice through the public network, but also be able to compare alternatives such as partial integration (just among the main nodes) or just the internal traffic.

We also can contemplate alternatives, such as integrating only the internal calls or using the private network to transport the external long-distance calls configuring the network to allow these calls getting through the public network in the node nearest to the destination. Another aspect that needs to be considered is that it may be economically feasible to do voice integration only between certain sites, excluding portions of the network.

We should proceed to identify the dynamic profile of the voice traffic in the same way we did when dealing with the data traffic. We must identify the dynamic voice traffic and, doing so, identify the discrete values (number of trunks and bandwidth) necessary to transport the calls.

When we do not have all the organization's bills, we should sample some specific trunks and, based on this sample, identify the voice traffic pattern. Based on this pattern and the number of people of each site, we then manage to identify the voice traffic of each site. When identifying the traffic interest based on samples, we must guarantee that the samples are representative of the organization's voice traffic interest.

Dynamical Volume Definition Strategy for Voice Traffic

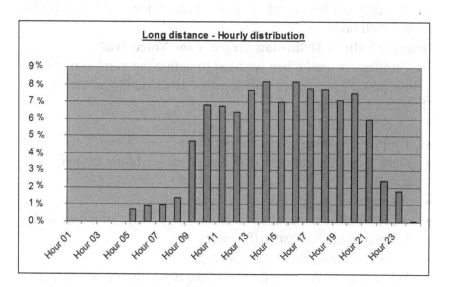

Here, we have a daily voice traffic distribution representing the average amount of spoken minutes and the corresponding percentage of spoken minutes per hour. This graphic was built and based on the telephone bills. We can usually get the telephone bills from the PTT in electronic format or through the internal billing system.

Based on the call logs, we identify the total spoken minutes per traffic generator unit (people). The visualization of the traffic volume over time is very important. It allows us to calculate the number of necessary trunks or necessary bandwidth (discrete volume) and adequately price the calls, given the fact that many countries charge different values for spoken minutes depending on the period of the day.

Voice tariff systems are typically based on volume (spoken minutes). Here it is noticeable that the layouts of the log files that the service providers provide vary a lot. Each service provider usually has its own format. Specialized consulting companies usually already have these layouts and are able to read these log files easily. However, if you are a telecommunications manager and do not have such layouts, you have to request them from your service providers. Generally speaking, we group the logs by time unit (usually per hour) and verify the percentage of the total traffic within each hour.

Discrete Volume Definition Strategy for Voice Traffic

This strategy is used when we need to define the number of circuits to transport a given voice traffic with a given quality of services. Our parameters are:

- People = Number of people per local
- Calls = Number of calls originated/received for each person per month
- Average = Average duration of each call
- TCF = Traffic concentration factor (percentage of the calls that happen in the busiest traffic hour)
- LOSS = Admissible loss/blocking[21]
- When setting the QoS for voice, we typically use between 1 and 5 percent as our maximum acceptable blocking (loss). When processing the raw data from the telephone bills, we typically use 21.2 as the average number of workdays per month. Therefore, based on our Erlang demand, we calculated how many trunks would be necessary to support the traffic with between 1 and 5 percent of blocking:
- (People × call × average)/(21.2) = Total calls day
- (Total calls day) × TCF = Total calls in the busiest hour in minutes
- (Total call in the busiest hours in minutes)/60 = number of Erlangs

Based on Erlang calculator programs, we identify the number of trunks using a defined blocking parameter (LOSS). Note that

21   We may use waiting time when calculating call centers.

the calculation can be based on loss (Erlang B) or retention (Erlang C). When calculating corporate networks, we use Erlang B. In case of call center, we use Erlang C. With the number of trunks, we are ready to calculate our voice load.

- Per = Percentage of the traffic that goes through the private network[22]
- Compression = Compression rate used by the private network to transport voice (typical values equals 8,16,32,64K)
- Voice load = Number of trunks × Per × Compression × 1024

Example of Voice Traffic Calculation Using the Dynamic Volume Definition Strategy

Here we have a typical company's office with sixty people. Based on the telephone bill, running the curve reader, we identify the average amount of spoken minutes and average number of calls for each person per day as well as the average daily total traffic. Here we identified 21,600 minutes per day. Each person gives an average of 72 calls per day with an average duration time per call of 5 minutes. The local PTT charges for the long-distance spoken minutes are based on two factors: location of the destination and period of the day when the call was placed.

Type of call	Spoken minute	Connection fee
Intra-LATA	USD 0,01	USD 0,10
Inter-LATA	USD 0,05	USD 0,10
International	Depends to where the call is destinated but in our example we are using USD 0,15	USD 0,10

The PTT had a discount system applicable, depending from when the call was done.

Time range	Discount applicable to the standard price
Between 1 AM and 6 AM	75%
Between 6 AM and 8 AM and 5 PM and 8 PM	50%
Between 8 AM and 9 AM, 12 AM and 1 PM and 4 PM and 5 PM	25%
Between 9 AM and 12 AM and 1 PM and 4 PM	Standard Price

Analyzing the call logs, we know the hourly distribution and produce an hourly calls distribution graphic.

---

22   It is used only when we are splitting the voice traffic between human attendants and IVRs.

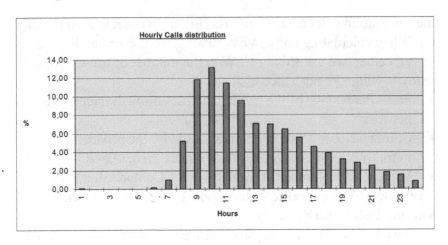

Therefore:

Time range	Discount applicable over the standard price	Percentage of our traffic in each time range
Between 1 AM and 6 AM	75%	0.20%
Between 6 AM and 8 AM and 5 PM and 8 PM	50%	21.2%
Between 8 AM and 9 AM, 12 AM and 1 PM and 4 PM and 5 PM	25%	26.8%
Between 9 AM and 12 AM and 1 PM and 4 PM	Normal price	51.8%

As can be seen in this example, in order to be able to identify the interconnection cost, it is absolutely crucial to know the hourly distribution and number of calls. So here we have to know the percentage of spoken minutes per person per each discount range for each application. When speaking about an application in this context (voice), we are speaking about types of voice calls such as local, long-distance, and international for each country. It is important to produce our traffic matrix in order to identify which flows we are willing to transport through our network. Consequently, we will use the chosen flows to calculate the bandwidths in an integrated voice/data structure.

At this point, we select the flows that represent a larger percentage of our costs. In our example, international calls to Brazil, England, and Argentina are the natural options, covering 79 percent of all voice costs.

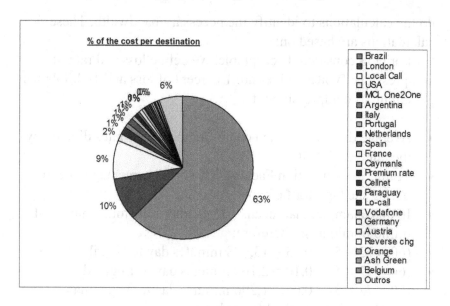

Note that it was possible to represent the traffic through a pizza graphic because we are analyzing only one site (one traffic unit). We select the flows representing the largest percentage of our costs. We are going to analyze these ones to determine if it is worth transporting through a private network. In this particular example, we selected the international calls to Brazil, Argentina, and England, encompassing 79 percent of our voice costs.

Range	Flow		Total	Percentage	Total day	Hourly distribution per range	Number of minutes	Number of calls	Price charge for the connection	Price charged	Total
Range-1	Voice to Brazil	21600	0.63	13608	0.002	27.216	5	0.5	1.02	1.52
Range-2	Voice to Brazil	21600	0.63	13608	0.212	2884.9	576	57.6	216.36	273.96
Range-3	Voice to Brazil	21600	0.63	13608	0.268	3646.9	729	72.9	410.28	483.18
Range-4	Voice to Brazil	21600	0.63	13608	0.518	7048.9	1409	140.9	1057.3	1198.2
Range-1	Voice to England	21600	0.1	2160	0.002	4.32	0	0	0.054	0.054
Range-2	Voice to England	21600	0.1	2160	0.212	457.92	91	9.1	11.44	20.54
Range-3	Voice to England	21600	0.1	2160	0.268	578.88	115	11.5	21.06	32.56
Range-4	Voice to England	21600	0.1	2160	0.518	1118.9	223	22.3	55.94	78.24
Range-1	Voice to Argentina	21600	0.06	1296	0.002	2.592	0	0	0.097	0.097
Range-2	Voice to Argentina	21600	0.06	1296	0.212	274.75	54	5.4	20.6	26
Range-3	Voice to Argentina	21600	0.06	1296	0.268	347.33	69	6.9	39.07	45.97
Range-4	Voice to Argentina	21600	0.06	1296	0.518	671.33	134	13.4	100.69	114.09

The spreadsheet demonstrates the current cost of each flow. In this example, we have a pricing strategy where calls have different prices depending on the time of the day. Once we select the flows that we are willing to transport through our network, we must do the calculations to identify the necessary bandwidth. These calculations are based on:

For QoS considered acceptable, we define loss and rate of compression. Typical values are 1 percent of loss and 16 kilobytes per circuit as compression rate.

- Average duration of each call = number of minutes divided by the number of calls
- Traffic Concentration Factor (TCF) = the percentage of calls during the high traffic hour
- In this example, that means 13 percent of the total amount of traffic in minutes. Therefore:
- $(60 \times 72 \times 5) \times 0.63 = 13,608$ minutes day to Brazil
- $(60 \times 72 \times 5) \times 0.10 = 2,160$ minutes day to England
- $(60 \times 72 \times 5) \times 0.06 = 1,296$ minutes day to Argentina
    The volume in the busiest hour:
- $(13,608) \times 0.13 = 1,769$ total minutes in the busiest hour to Brazil
- $(2,160) \times 0.13 = 280.80$ total minutes in the busiest hour to England
- $(1,296) \times 0.13 = 168.48$ total minutes in the busiest hour to Argentina
    The number of necessary Erlangs:
- $(1769.00)/60 = 29.48$ number of Erlangs necessary to Brazil
- $(280.80)/60 = 4.68$ number of Erlangs necessary to England
- $(168.48)/60 = 2.80$ number of Erlangs necessary to Argentina

Using the Erlang calculators, we identify the number of necessary trunks given a number of Erlangs. Assume a defined blocking parameter (LOSS = 1 percent). (See Erlang calculators in chapter nineteen.)

The result of our Erlang calculator for this particular example:

- 36 trunks necessary to Brazil
- 8 trunks necessary to England
- 4 trunks necessary to Argentina

With the number of trunks, we are ready to calculate our voice load based on the compression rate per voice channel. That means the necessary bandwidth per channel.

- Compression = Compression rate used in our private network to transport voice (typical values of 8,16,32,64K)[23]
- Voice load = Number of trunks × Compression × 1,024

  With these parameters, we do the calculations as follows:

Name	calculated necessary Erlangs	Number of trunks = Loss 1%	Bandwidth assuming 16K per channel
Voice to Brazil	29,48	36	576
Voice to England	4,68	8	128
Voice to Argentine	2,8	4	64

Now we know the necessary bandwidth to be added to the data network to support the voice flows. Of course, we have to correlate these volumes with the bandwidth cost for each connection and evaluate if this cost is smaller than just letting the calls go through the public network. In large networks, these calculations are hard, depending on the size of the network even impossible to do without deploying analytical tools.

14.1.4 Hardware Already in Use (Capacities and Costs)

Now that we already have the traffic mapped, we have to identify the hardware in use by the organization, including models and capacities of PBXs, routers, and switches. This is an important part of the process. Depending on which hardware the organization uses and how it is contracted and deployed, the strategy for designing the new network may change. A good example here would be a situation where the organization owns all hardware. In this scenario, we must direct our effort to try to maximize this investment as much as possible.

14.1.5 Miscellaneous Information

23 In our example, we defined 16K as the necessary bandwidth by voice channel.

The necessary information may vary, but, in general, to understand the organization's current situation in terms of telecommunications, we need to identify the following information besides mapping the traffic and identifying the hardware:

- Identify the current number of trunks and extensions in each site
- Identify the current topology (how the connections are linked)
- Identify all interconnections contracted by the organization to all service providers, including costs and bandwidths
- Identify all maintenance, leasing, and rent costs
- Identify the personnel costs (internal and external)

Having all information listed above, we will know exactly what the current telecommunications expenditures are. In addition, we also have to understand the following aspects:

- If the current network integrates voice and data
- If the current topology is compatible with the tariff system
- If the bandwidths are properly calculated
- If the organization is paying the adequate value for maintenance/rent and personnel
- If the organization manages its telecommunications resources properly
- If contingency plans are in place

All this information together will give us a clear understanding of where the organization is today in terms of the deployment of telecommunications resources.

14.2 Information Regarding the Environment

When planning a telecommunications network, as when planning a logistical network, we must understand the environment where the transport of our traffic will happen. Transportation environments have modals, transport companies, geographic locations, costs of transport, and available routes. These elements apply to both logistical networks that transport goods and data networks that transport data and voice. In a logistical network, the modals available are maritime, aerial, or terrestrial. In the telecommunications network, these are the technologies available. The analogy holds for all environmental elements. The transport companies are service providers, locations of distribution warehouses are aggregation nodes, transport cost is the tariffs, and available routes are the infrastructure available. Note that the modal affects which routes are available in telecommunications networks, just as in materials logistics networks. There are additional considerations, too. Do you buy a ship and operate it, or do you pay a shipping company by volume transported? This can be seen as an access strategy decision for the network. Based on this analogy, we can easily identify which environmental information is necessary to properly plan a telecommunications network. We can group this information into seven types:

- Potential aggregation nodes
- Interconnection costs
- Potential service providers
- Interconnection technologies available
- Access strategy alternatives
- Hardware and infrastructure costs
- Routes available

14.2.1 Potential Aggregation Nodes

Here we have to identify all sites available to be used as aggregation nodes (see chapter three). The algorithms to be discussed subsequently will select which sites will be more suitable to be used as aggregation nodes. Such selection will happen within a group of predefined sites.

We use algorithms to create topological scenarios where the number and location of the nodes will vary. These scenarios are defined by varying the minimum traffic volume, which makes the existence of an aggregation node feasible.

Therefore, if we were planning a corporate WAN and the organization had as an operational policy to maintain all transport equipment within its own sites, we define the organization's sites as the potential traffic aggregation nodes. On the other hand, if we had the possibility of installing the transport equipment within the service providers COs, we could consider the service providers COs as potential traffic aggregation nodes.

14.2.2 Interconnection Costs

When planning a WAN, having a complete view of the interconnection costs is absolutely crucial. It is important to know the cost to transport our data and voice flows among our traffic units (sites). We must be able to calculate the costs associated with the several possible topologies identifying the cost to interconnect the aggregation nodes (backbone) and cost to connect the traffic units to the aggregation nodes (access). In this item, we will explain how these calculations are executed, assuming we are going to prepare specific programs (interconnection cost calculators) to execute these calculations. Nevertheless, in some cases, calculations may be done manually if the size of the network allows.

Whether we are going to build our own infrastructure or contract it from somebody, the interconnection costs will always be there, and we should be able to identify them. In the majority of the cases, we do not have to have all connection costs to produce a reasonable analysis. We can infer the rules defining the costs based on samples. For example, not having all interconnection costs among the sites and having some difficulty to get these costs from the service provider, it is perfectly acceptable from the precision standpoint to infer the pricing rules based on a small sample. This inference is done through using nonlinear regression and interpolation techniques.

This information enables us to calculate the ideal structure. One positive aspect is the fact that, once having a chance to do this kind of analysis in a given area, these costs can be deployed to support other projects within the same area.

The interconnection cost calculators are tailor-made programs, which, based on the required volume (discrete or dynamic) and in the endpoints A and B, identify the interconnection costs. They are instrumental when doing these calculations in large networks with multiple alternatives in terms of topology. In large projects, when having many possible interconnection provider alternatives, we may use more than one interconnection cost calculator. Doing so, we can identify which kind of technology and service provider is ideal for each interconnection or which service provider has the smaller total cost.

So we have to identify the rules that the service providers adopted to define the prices of the several services. Usually, the service providers do not make available the formulas used to define their prices. Such formulas would allow the identification of the variables influencing the prices and how they are correlated. Most often, we have to infer this formula through reverse engineering based on its results (the prices).

Interconnection costs can follow many different pricing structures. The volume (discrete or dynamic), distance, and extremities of the connection should usually be enough to allow us to identify the price to be paid for the interconnection. As can be seen in the examples:

- **PTT lease lines:** Typically follows a function correlating distance × volumes (bandwidths)
- **Fiber optical infrastructure:** Usually represented as a distance function and number of derivations
- **Satellite interconnection:** Usually the cost reflects the volumes in/out and number of dishes deployed
- **Dial-up access:** Normally follows a PTT price spreadsheet widely known.

These are usually the variables influencing the price: bandwidth (nominal, CIR, and EIR); distance; transported kilobits; spoken minutes; and hourly distribution. Although we do find situations where other variables are influencing the prices, we can affirm with reasonable confidence that, in most cases, those are the variables defining the price. To identify the pricing rule, we should follow two steps:

- Identify which parameters are actually influencing the prices.

- Identify the formula correlating the parameters identified as influencing the price.

We should not forget the applicable taxes. Even though taxes are not exactly a parameter, it is a factor to be verified.

14.2.2.1 Identifying the Parameters Influencing the Price

If two variables have a correlation of cause and effect (one varies and the other also varies), we say that these variables are correlated. Our objective is to try to map which variables are correlated with the price of a service. Once done, we exactly establish this correlation.

So the basic objective of the following technique is to measure the relationship between two given variables that we suspect may be linked by a cause-and-effect correlation. The level of this relationship can be measured by the expression:

- Consider $X1, X2, X3 \ldots Xn$ as a sequence of values of a given variable (for example, bandwidth)
- Consider $Y1, Y2, Y3 \ldots Yn$ as the values of the other variable (for example, cost)
- Assume x_m, y_m, δx, and δy as the average and standard deviation of the two groups of values

To be able to identify the level of association and correlation coefficient (R), $R = \delta xy / \Delta x \delta y$, where $\delta xy = \Sigma(x_i - x_m)(y_i - y_m) = \Sigma x_i y_i - n x_m y_m$ $n-1$ $n-1$.

Assume the following values in a correlation (bandwidth versus cost): $n = 18$, $x_m = 0.48$, $y_m = 1.58$, $\delta x = 0.18$, $\delta y = 0.54$, and $\Sigma x_i y_i = 12.44$. Based on that, we identify $R = -0.079$. A Greek letter defines what we call population correlation coefficient (ρ). We can consider R as the estimative of ρ, exactly as x_m is an estimative of population average ρ. We can subsequently see the Pearson coefficient correlation:

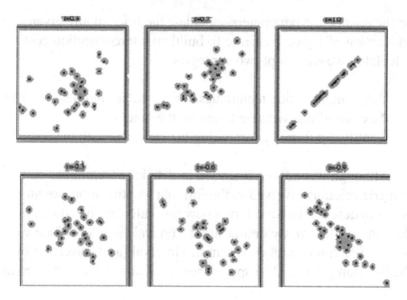

Determination Coefficient (R²)

The Pearson coefficient correlation elevated to the square is called *determination coefficient*, or only R^2. It is a measure of the variability proportion between two variables. It is very uncommon to find a perfect correlation ($R^2 = 1$) because there are usually several factors determining the relationship between variables in the real world.

In our example, if we had $R = -0.79$, therefore $R^2 = 0.62$, or 62 percent. That means that 38 percent of the cost variance cannot be described or explained due to the variance of the bandwidth and vice versa. So it becomes clear that other factors are influencing the price, for example, distance, CIR, and so forth.

Once we defined there is a correlation between two variables and this correlation is representative, we must build a model that will allow us to replicate the values of a variable (cost for example) based on other values. For these models (programs), we give the name of interconnection cost calculators.

14.2.2.2 Identifying Formula Correlating Parameters with Cost

Once we identified the variables influencing the price, we build interconnection cost calculators. These are programs that, based on the connection parameters, calculate the price of any given connection of a given service. To build an interconnection cost calculator, we can adopt two strategies:

- Using interpolation techniques and based on samples, identify the costs of one variable based on the other *or*
- Identify the formula correlating the variables with the cost

Although it is not our intention to detail the techniques of numeric calculus involved in the formula identification, we are going to describe in basic terms how this calculation is done. In the example below, we demonstrate a typical situation where we have only a finite number of samples interval [a,b] correlated by the function y = f(x). The spreadsheet correlates bandwidth versus cost.

Bandwidth Kbits/s	64K x	Monthly cost
2048	32	R$ 8.770,00
- 1024	16	R$ 5.350,00
512	8	R$ 2.830,00
256	4	R$ 1.560,00
128	2	R$ 1.000,00
64	1	R$ 650,00

In this case, our objective is to identify the cost for any given bandwidth. As mentioned, we have two possible alternatives:

- Using the interpolation techniques, make the approximation of the values of Y based on a given value of X *or*
- Identify the exact formula correlating the variable's bandwidth and cost

Option One: Interpolation

In this example, we have twenty-eight samples. Based on these samples, we are able to determine the price of any connection, regardless of the bandwidth. We usually use a technique known as Lagrange interpolation when building our interconnection cost calculators based on interpolation. The bigger the number of samples, the more accurate the results are. Such programs are tailor-made and allow us to identify the interconnection costs (backbone or access) based on the parameters influencing the price of a given service. We usually have to prepare such programs to each potential service considered as an alternative. For example:

```
* PROGRAM : Lagrange.prg

* WRITTEN BY: Luiz Augusto de Carvalho

* Date : 05/19/2002

* Objective : Lagrange Interpolation

****************************************************************************************
**

* Nmax = Maximum number of points declared * N = Spreadsheet maximum number of
points

* NPI = Number of points to be interpolated * X = Vector that contains the abscissa of the
points interpolated

* y = Vector that contains the ordinates of the points interpolated

parc = 0.00000000000;nmax = 28;npi = 1 && number of points to be identified;n = 28 &&
number of samples ;dimension tabela(nmax,2)

dimension x(nmax)

dimension y(nmax)

tabela (1,1) = 0;tabela (2,1) = 12.816;tabela (3,1) = 50;tabela (4,1) = 100;tabela (5,1) =
166.608;abela (6,1) = 250

tabela (7,1) = 333.216;abela (8,1) = 485.406;abela (9,1) = 676.044;abela (10,1) =
825.03;tabela (11,1) = 1000;tabela (12,1) = 1200

tabela (13,1) = 1700;tabela (14,1)= 2200;tabela (15,1) = 2500;tabela (16,1) = 2600;tabela
(17,1) = 2800;tabela (18,1) = 2900

tabela (19,1) = 1900;tabela (20,1) = 2702.574;tabela (21,1) = 3100;tabela (22,1) =
3200;tabela (23,1) = 3351.384;tabela (24,1) = 3450

tabela (25,1) = 3500;tabela (26,1) = 3900;tabela (27,1) = 1500;tabela (28,1) =
2000;tabela (1,2) = 580;tabela (2,2) = 656.8;tabela (3,2) = 610;tabela (4,2) = 650;tabela
(5,2) = 570;tabela (6,2) = 800;tabela (7,2) = 920;tabela (8,2) = 1038;tabela (9,2) =
1009;tabela (10,2) = 1297.75;tabela (11,2) = 1300;tabela (12,2) = 1400;tabela (13,2)
= 1600;tabela (14,2) = 1675;tabela (15,2) = 1700;tabela (16,2) = 1725;tabela (17,2) =
1750;tabela (18,2) = 1800;tabela (19,2) = 1620;tabela (20,2) = 1881.75;tabela (21,2) =
1850;tabela (22,2) = 1870;tabela (23,2) = 1983;tabela (24,2) = 1890;tabela (25,2) = 1895
;tabela (26,2) = 1905;tabela (27,2) = 1500;tabela (28,2) = 1650

x(1)=2700

for k = 1 to Npi
 y(k) =0.00000000
```

```
for I = 1 to n

parc = 1.000000

for j = 1 to N

if i<>j

parc = parc*(x(k)-tabela(j,1))/(tabela(i,1)-tabela(j,1))

endif

next j

y(k) = y(k)+parc*tabela(I,2)

? parc, "parc", y(k), "y(k)"

next I

? "************************************"

? K, x(k), y(k)

* @ k,1 say " "+str(y(k),8,4)

next k
```

Option Two: Identifying the Formula

Having the discrete values, we can identify how the variables influencing the prices correlate these with each other and the price. In other words, we identify the formula generating the prices. We do that through nonlinear regression techniques. Through these techniques, we identify the polynomial correlating these variables (distance, bandwidth, duration, CIR, and so forth). For example:

```
* PROGRAM : EQ4.prg

* WRTTEN BY: Luiz Augusto de Carvalho

* DATE : 06/02/2002

* OBJECTIVE : Non-linear regression

********************************************************************

set talk off

tot1=100000000000000000000000000

tot=100

@ 0,1 clear to 20,80

a = -1000;b = -1000;c = -1000;d = -1000;e = -1000

aa = 1000;bb = 1000;cc = 1000;dd = 1000;ee = 1000

aaa = a;bbb = b;ccc = c;ddd = d;eee = e

do while round(tot,2)<>0

increa=(abs(aaa)+aa)

increb=(abs(bbb)+bb)

increc=(abs(ccc)+cc)

incred=(abs(ddd)+dd)

incree=(abs(eee)+ee)

*? aaa,aa,bbb,bb,ccc,cc,ddd,dd,eee,ee

*wait

a=aaa

*? a, aa, aaa

*wait

do while aa>=a

a=a+increa

b=bbb

do while bb>=b
```

```
b=b+increb

c=ccc

do while cc>=c

c=c+increc

d=ddd

do while dd>=d

d=d+incred

e=eee

do while ee>=e

*? increa,increb,increc,incred,incree

*? a,b,c,d,e

e=e+incree

store (19153437143296*a)+(9155562688*b)+(4376464*c)+(2092*d)+e-1258.93 to
formula1

store (8042079252736*a)+(4775581504*b)+(2835856*c)+(1684*d)+e-1196.26 to
formula2

store (70344300625*a)+(136590875*b)+(265225*c)+(515*d)+e-754.56 to formula3

store (24343800625*a)+(61629875*b)+(156025*c)+(395*d)+e-678.66 to formula4

store (38416*a)+(2744*b)+(196*c)+(14*d)+e-107.52 to formula5

store Abs(formula1)+abs(formula2)+abs(formula3)+abs(formula4)+abs(formula5) to tot

enddo

enddo

enddo

enddo

enddo

@ 09,05 say "O resultado menor foi : "+str(tot1,30,10)+" "+str(incree,10,5)

@ 10,05 say "incre a: "+str(increa,10,3)+" incre b: "+str(increb,10,3)+" incre c:
"+str(increc,10,3)

@ 11,05 say "incre d: "+str(incred,10,3)+" Incre e: "+str(incree,10,3)
```

```
*if tot<tot1

*? a, aa, aaa

*wait

*if a=aaa

* aa = aa-(abs(aaa)+aa)/4

*else

* aaa=aaa+(abs(aaa)+aa)/4
*endif
* if b=bbb

* bb=bb-(abs(bbb)+bb)/4

* else

* bbb=bbb+(abs(bbb)+bb)/4

* endif

* if c=ccc

* cc =cc-(abs(ccc)+cc)/4

* else

* ccc = ccc+(abs(ccc)+cc)/4

* endif

* if d=ddd

* dd=dd-(abs(ddd)+dd)/4

*else

* ddd=ddd+(abs(ddd)+dd)/4

*endif

*if e=eee

* ee=ee-(abs(eee)+ee)/4

*else

* eee=eee+(abs(eee)+ee)/4

*endif
```

```
*increa = (abs(aaa)+aa)

*increb = (abs(bbb)+bb)

*increc = (abs(ccc)+cc)

*incred = (abs(ddd)+dd)

*incree = (abs(eee)+ee)

*else

aa = aa-.01

aaa = aaa+.01

bb = bb-.01

bbb = bbb+.01

cc = cc-.01

ccc = ccc+.01

dd = dd-.01

ddd= ddd+.01

ee = ee-.01

eee = eee+.01

increa = (abs(aaa)+aa)

increb = (abs(bbb)+bb)

increc = (abs(ccc)+cc)

incred = (abs(ddd)+dd)

incree = (abs(eee)+ee)

*endif

if tot<tot1

store tot to tot1

store a to a1

store b to b1

store c to c1

store d to d1
```

```
store e to e1

@ 1,1 say " "+str(a1,20,10)+"X4+"+str(b1,20,10)+"X3+"+str(c1,20,10)+"X2+"

@ 2,1 say " "+str(d1,20,10)+"X+"+str(e1,20,10)+"="+str(tot1,30,10)
endif

enddo
```

This program solves a fourth-level polynomial. Once we build these interconnection cost calculators, we can test several topologies and volumes quickly.

14.2.3 Interconnection Technologies

We can use several technologies to provide connectivity between our sites. We should research which ones are available in the area analyzed, identify their pricing models, and load their costs in our interconnection and hardware cost calculators.

Note that we can include or exclude the premises equipment in our access cost and can associate (or not) the type of our access with the hardware deployed in the nodes. For instance, if we are performing an analysis for a service provider and decide to implement ADSL as our access alternative, we would have to link this choice with the deployment of DSLAMs in the nodes. On the other hand, if we are analyzing an enterprise network and ADSL is one of the alternatives of last mile access, we would not need to associate the use of this alternative with the deployment of DSLAMs in the nodes. In this case, from our perspective, the ADSL is just a possible interconnection service, and the DSLAM is part of the service provider cloud. In fact, each case should be analyzed carefully, always separating what part belongs to the network analyzed and what part can be considered only as interconnection or cloud.

When analyzing a structure, we should never lose track that the important concept is the interconnection cost to support a given demand. Therefore, if, for example, we have an ATM or frame-relay interconnection and the service provider charges based on the volume of packets, we have to adjust our model to calculate our volume based in packets. We should build an interconnection cost calculator to support this particular scenario. As long we manage to do the necessary adjustments, the process will work well, regardless of the technology deployed.

14.2.4 Access Strategy Alternatives

When defining what strategy should be deployed to provide the access (understanding access as the connection between sites and nodes), we often face two basic kinds of possibilities: permanent and volume-based access or dedicated and switched.

Both approaches have pros and cons, and it is highly recommended to include both in the interconnection cost calculators. The costs, network volume, and hourly distribution will define which strategy is more adequate. Bringing this decision for a more practical perspective, here we have to decide things such as whether or not to contract a leased line paid on a monthly basis or a packet network paid by number of packets transported.

If we measure our volumes in hourly slots, we have a clear view of how our traffic varies during the day, and we know the exact amount of traffic to be transported. Having this information, we can compare the cost of transporting the traffic on a per unit basis (bits/s or minutes) in a usage-based pricing strategy (using the dynamical volume) with paying defined monthly fees for permanent interconnections with defined bandwidth (discrete volume). In general, the more sporadic the traffic profile, the more attractive volume-based connections tends to be. Of course, it is impossible to generalize, and each case should be properly calculated.

Due to the possibilities described, it is sometimes worth splitting the voice and data traffic in the access (our dial-up access). Voice is traditionally charged based on usage (volume) and, in some cases, not charged at all, for example, when interconnecting points inside the same area code in Canada and United States. In situations like that, obviously, the usage-based pricing alternative becomes extremely attractive.

When treating the issue of voice integration, we can also adopt partial solutions. For instance, in a corporate network, we may decide to do this integration just among the backbone nodes. In this situation, the office's external voice traffic will be carried by the PTT infrastructure, going through the company's backbone only when the cost to perform the entire call through the PTT surpasses the interconnection cost to the nearest node. So we could divide the alternatives into two. We can adopt a fully integrated strategy.

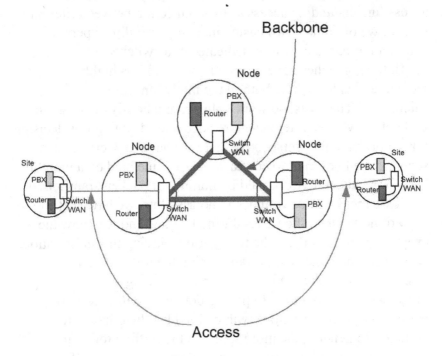

In this example, all internal traffic flows entirely through the private infrastructure.

In the partial solution, the strategy would be different.

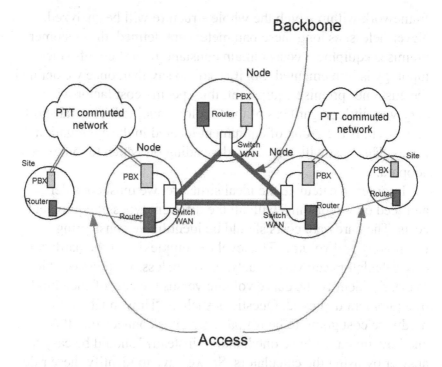

The partial strategy is especially attractive in countries where no fees are charged by the PTT for calls within the same area code.

14.2.5 Hardware Cost

When designing a network, we can divide the devices involved in basically two groups: customer premises equipment and transport equipment. The customer premises equipment can be very diverse, and the option chosen depends on two basic factors: the volume (in/out) and protocols required. Of course, when mentioning these two factors, we are treating the issue from the technical perspective only. In the real world, in most cases, current infrastructure and contracts, costs, and public infrastructure availability count as much as the two aspects mentioned before. In general, we can easily identify the alternatives available in a given area and select which ones would be feasible to be deployed by each site and set them as possible alternatives.

The type of technology deployed in each site will be determined by the structure of the network and will define the framework within which the whole structure will be analyzed. Nevertheless, as long these parameters are defined, the customer premises equipment costs remain constant, regardless of which topology is implemented. So, it is safe to say that, once we defined the customer premise equipment, this specific cost factor will vary very little, regardless of the topology adopted. The transport equipment is the group of equipment located in the aggregation nodes. This cost will vary a lot, depending on which topology is adopted.

In order to calculate the ideal structure, we must consider and feed our algorithms with all the different types of equipment costs. The hardware costs should be identifiable considering technology and volume. The level of complexity of the hardware cost calculators can vary widely. Nevertheless, we must be able to clearly identify the curve volume versus the cost of each kind of equipment deployed. Questions such as "How much is my hardware cost going to be if I have ten sites connected to this node and how much if I have one hundred instead?" should be easy to answer by using the calculators. So we have to identify these rules and load them into the algorithms.

14.2.5.1 Hardware Cost Calculators

Hardware cost calculators are tailor-made software through which we can identify the cost of each kind of hardware based in a given volume. This volume can be: number of sites, people or workstations connected to the node, and total traffic volume in/out flowing through the node. When defining the hardware cost calculator, the first step is to identify which equipment is going to be deployed in the nodes defined as a typical node. The second step is establishing the interrelation among the hardware. Examples of typical nodes:

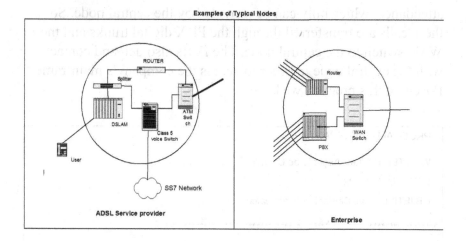

Examples of Typical Nodes

Here we will simulate a very simple hardware cost calculator, just to give the reader a general view. Real hardware cost calculators are usually much more complex and involve many other details. Here we are designing a call center structure to collect traffic. This is our typical node:

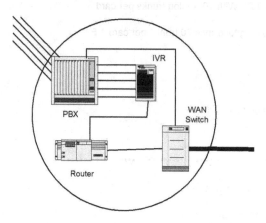

In this example our typical node basically includes four types of equipment: PBX, IVR, router, and WAN switch. These devices are dimensioned based on the number of calls received. (This is an inbound-only call center.) With the number of calls, we calculate the number of trunks necessary in the PBX. The incoming calls are always transferred first to the IVR, and 40 percent of them are terminated there. However, 60 percent of them demand human attendance, which only can be provided by the central node. So these calls are transferred through the PBX digital trunks and the WAN switch to the central node. The IVRs also demand contact with the central node in order to access the company's mainframe. Based on this process, we have:

```
* PROGRAM : PRICEHAR1.prg

* WRITTEN BY: Luiz Augusto de Carvalho

* DATE : 06/02/2002

* OBJETIVE : Call-Center hardware calculator

*********************************************************************

* Calculating PBX cost

*********************************************************************

PBXhack=10000 && PBX rack supporting 20 cards into two shelves

Extensioncard=1000 && With 32 extensions each

analogcard=2400 && With 16 Analog trunks per card

digcard=1800 && Digital trunks 30 trunks per card 1 E1

ntrunks= 200

ncards=0

* PBX - Calculation *

* Analog trunks *

*********************************************************************

ntrunkcard=int(ntrunks/16)+1

Ncards=ncards+ntrunkcard

ptrunkcard=ntrunkcard*analogcard

* Digital trunks

*********************************************************************

ndigtrunks=int(ntrunks*0.6)+1 && 60 percent calls need human attendance
```

```
if (ndigtrunks/30)-int(ndigtrunks/30)<>0

ndigcard= int(ndigtrunks/30)+1

else

ndigcard= int(ndigtrunks/30)

endif

pdigcard=ndigcard*digcard

Ncards=ncards+ndigcard

* Extensions *

**********************************************************************

nextension=Ntrunks

if (nextension/32)-int(nextension/32)<>0

nextcard= int(nextension/32)+1

else

nextcard= int(nextension/32)

endif

pext=nextcard*extensioncard

ncards=ncards+nextcard

* Magazine PBX *

**********************************************************************

if (ncards/40)-int(ncards/40)<>0

nhack= int(ncards/40)+1

else

nhack= int(ncards/40)

endif

phack=nhack*pbxhack

pbxprice=phack+ptrunkcard+pdigcard+pext

* IVR Calculation *
```

```
*********************************************************************

pivrhack=800 && IVR hack cost with 6 slots for cards each

ivrtrunk = 70 && Card with 8 trunks each

nivrcard=int(ntrunks/8)+1

if (nivrcard/6)-int(nivrcard/6)<>0

nivrhack= int(nivrcard/6)+1

else

nivrhack= int(nivrcard/6)

endif

pivr=(ivrtrunk*nivrcard)+(pivrhack*nivrhack)

? pivr

* WAN switch Calculation *

*********************************************************************

pcard1=1500

pcard2=500

switchhack=20000

nswitch=ndigcard+1

nswitch=2*nswitch

if (nswitch/16)-int(nswitch/16)<>0

nswitchhack= int(nswitch/16)+1

else

nswitchhack= int(nswitch/16)

endif

pswitch=(switchhack*nswitchhack)+(nswitch*(pcard1+pcard2))

? pswitch

* ROUTER Calculation *
```

```
***********************************************************************

router = 2500 && router CISCO 2509 US$ 2500

? "Total price = ", str((pbxprice+pivr+pswitch+router),10,2)

* montly rate .05 including maintainance


? "Total monthly price = ", str(((pbxprice+pivr+pswitch+router)*.05),10,2)
```

In careful analysis, we build detailed hardware cost calculators. Depending on the complexity of the project, we can even include many possible vendors. Including more than one possible vendor allows us to determine both the ideal structure and preferred vendor.

The results calculated by the hardware cost calculators should provide monthly-based costs, covering the complete ownership cost, including equipment, maintenance, and management. We must decide which percentage of the cost will be considered. Typical values are [24]:

Cost item	Monthly % of the buying cost
Maintenance	1%
Management	0.5%
Leasing for five years	3%

These financial parameters must be defined when preparing the hardware cost calculator and should be identified in the market where the equipment will be ordered, being as close as possible to the real market practice and the WACC of the organization.

14.2.6 Routes Available

---

24 These values can vary a lot depending where you are in the world and the economical environment, our intention is just to give you a reference that may be valid within the Americas.

Another important factor to be identified is the availability of interconnections among the traffic units (sites). In an ideal world, all sites could be connected directly to the others. However, the reality shows that, in most cases, we must adapt our planning to a very limited number of interconnection alternatives, usually limited to the public infrastructure available. And even when we are willing to build our own interconnections, some routes are not feasible. In other words, when performing this calculation, we can assume that all nodes can be connected to each other without constraints or constraints can be introduced based on our knowledge of the real interconnections possibilities.

The first step is to identify the interconnection available, mapping the public infrastructure available and therefore avoiding the possibility of Considering in our calculations routes which are not available. Another important aspect when mapping the infrastructure is the definition of reasonable routes. For instance, if we want to connect two cities in Brazil (São Paulo and Rio de Janeiro), we may limit the hops in order to avoid routes that are too long. In most cases, the service providers themselves will inform their coverage area, routes, and points of presence. The following is the coverage area of a service provider within São Paulo city area:

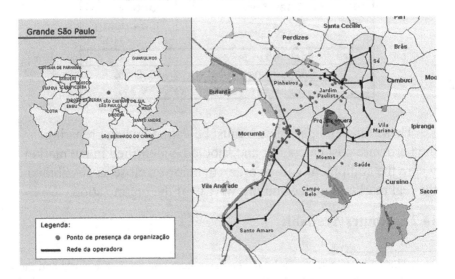

212

Explaining it in other way, when executing these calculations, we can assume that all nodes can be connected among themselves without constraints or introduce limitations based on our knowledge of the real possibilities. In some global environments, a mesh might well be possible via technologies such as MPLS and NNI agreements between carriers. However, certain countries are still highly regulated, for example, Russia. Additionally, it makes sense to distribute major services to different regions of the world due to latency and performance or other political constraints.

14.3 *Nonexclusive Information*

In addition to information specific to the organization, a wealth of nonexclusive information can influence decisions regarding a WAN. Nonexclusive information includes:

- All information that can be used as valid reference in the absence of specific data
- Parameters defined based on our understanding of what is the ideal QoS

So, depending on which specific information is available to execute a project, we may need to use more or less nonexclusive information. For example, if we do not have precise measurements, we can use traffic patterns of organizations with similar operational patterns.

For the same reason, if we do not have specific quotations of interconnections or hardware, we may use nonexclusive information received through quotations done in other organizations within the same area. This type of possibility drives services of specialized consulting companies. They are able to provide typical parameters and nonexclusive information to bridge information gaps. The other category of nonexclusive information is the parameters:

- We usually execute the calculations using a voice loss pattern of 1 percent.

- We usually execute the calculations using an overhead for IP encapsulating of 5 percent.

When identifying these parameters, it is common that unrealistic expectations about the QoS desired are set. Most times, this unrealistic expectation is motivated by the lack of understanding of the correlation between cost and performance. The definition about the adequate QoS of each application has to be based on the tolerance of each application used by the organization. When defining the parameters and doing the calculations, we must have a clear view about the implications in terms of costs and benefits.

Confronted with these problems, we can adopt several strategies from precise measurements to reverse calculation based on nonexclusive information (inferences). The ideal strategy is specific for each situation.

15

Generating the Designs

Once we have the necessary data, now it is time to design the network. In this chapter, we will discuss how to execute an effective design. Getting a design that works is important, but it is not enough. Designing an overengineered network is not difficult. The true challenge lies in the design of an optimal structure that minimizes cost while maximizing performance.

As already discussed, the problems that a WAN designer face are basically logistic. For instance, most organizations need to find the best possible location for their offices, manufacturers, and warehouses. A bad location will be translated into higher costs and lower competitiveness. The same concepts apply to the telecommunications networks. Bad logistic arrangements will generate higher costs.

In this chapter, we will describe how to design WANs deploying tools. In our view, properly designing a large WAN and doing all the necessary calculations manually is virtually impossible. Tools are required even for small, relatively simple networks. The tools created to help design a WAN allow the automated planning of several types of telecommunications networks.

The algorithms deployed by these tools are publicly known. It is not our objective to discuss the codes of such algorithms, but the concepts used by them and how to deploy them. The concepts described in this book can be implemented in several ways. To find samples of such codes, see the bibliographic reference. We will describe briefly the several classes of algorithms and the problems addressed by them. The WAN design algorithms can be divided into several classes depending on the type of problem. We can consider basically the following classes:

- Minimum spanning tree (MST)
- Constrained minimum spanning tree (CMST)
- Smaller/cheaper route
- Node location identifiers
- Site associations
- Optimum routing
- Capacity planners
- Meshed networks
- Interconnection cost calculators

This book deals with the logic supporting the algorithms, not the algorithms themselves. Such analyses demand a thorough data gathering. Only after getting the necessary information (chapter fourteen), we can initiate the analytical process. The analytical process typically encompasses two phases: generating topological scenarios and testing all topological scenarios using the interconnection costs available. All the tools presented in the bibliographic reference will somehow follow the logics described here. We recommend you read this chapter before trying to understand the codes themselves.

The process of identifying the ideal structure is based on the following concept. A network can vary from a complete centralized structure (star topology) to a complete distributed one. The following example gives a conceptual view about how the creation of the topological scenarios occurs.

Here we have a network with twenty remote sites and one data center. When analyzing the structure, we vary the number of sites, which makes the existence of telecommunications aggregation nodes feasible from one to twenty. Doing that, we identify all possible topologies. Together, with the interconnection costs, we can calculate which one (topology) produces the cheapest design.

- One site is enough to justify the creation of a telecommunications aggregation node. In this example, we have:
  - Backbone cost = X = Maximum (dark grey)
  - Access cost = Y = 0
  - Node hardware cost = W = 0
  - Total network cost = X + Y + W

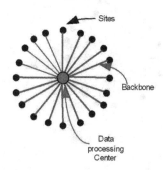

- Ten sites are enough to justify the creation of a telecommunications aggregation node. In this example, we have:
  - Backbone cost = X (dark grey)
  - Access cost = Y (light grey)
  - Node hardware cost = W (black)
  - Total network cost = X + Y + W

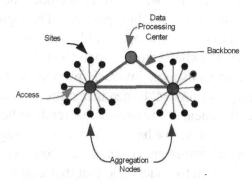

- Twenty nodes are enough to create a telecommunications aggregation node. In this example, we have:
  - Backbone cost = X =0
  - Access cost = Y = Maximum (light grey)
  - Node Hardware cost = W = 0
  - Total network cost = X + Y + W

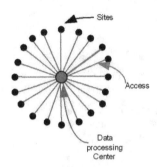

As can be seen in the examples above, we have three basic elements in a network structure:

- **Access:** The connection between the traffic source (site/end user) to an aggregation node
- **Backbone:** The interconnections among the aggregation nodes
- **Node hardware:** Hardware necessary in the aggregation nodes

The more cost-effective WAN will be the one where the sum of these three factors is the smallest possible. The logic of this analysis is shown in the following formula: Access Costs + Node Hardware Costs + Backbone Cost = Total Cost

The access cost tends to be inversely proportional to the number of aggregation nodes. It means that the more aggregation nodes we have, the cheaper the access cost tends to be. On the other hand, the more sites we have linked to an aggregation node, the bigger the node's hardware cost and backbone cost tends to be.

Here it is important to understand that this kind of problem is a heuristic problem. That means it is a problem to which we do not have only one possible solution, but several. This is why operational and management factors are so important to complement the process of choosing the best design.

Our challenge is to identify which combination of these three factors will produce the more cost-effective solution. We find this ideal point through exhaustive search, calculating all possible scenarios, and going from a complete star topology where the backbone cost is zero to a complete distributed structure where the access cost is zero. Physically, these two extremes will look exactly the same.

15.1 Topological Scenarios Generation

The first step is to determine how many and where the aggregation nodes are (backbone definition). In this phase, our network will include two distinct groups of structural entities: the aggregation nodes (backbone) and traffic units (sites/group of sources of traffic).

Using a hybrid algorithm, such as Prim-Dijkstra, the backbone nodes will be connected among themselves. The traffic units will be connected to the nearest node in a star topology (access).

The topology generators algorithms define which traffic volume makes the existence of an aggregation node feasible. Applying these tools involves varying this volume from a minimum amount (a workstation, for example) to the total network volume. Proceeding in this way, the algorithm manages to generate all topologies from a complete distributed to a complete centralized network. These two extremes are reached in the following two scenarios:

- If we assume the minimum volume to justify an existence of a network as the traffic generated by a traffic unit (assuming all traffic units have the same traffic volume), the topology will be completely distributed, and the cost situation will be minimum access cost and maximum backbone cost.
- If we assume the number of sites to make our node feasible is equal to the total number of traffic units (sites), the topology will be completely centralized in only one node, and the cost

situation will be minimum backbone cost and maximum access cost.

- These two extremes can be defined in terms of cost driver:
- Completely distributed networks have access cost minimum/ backbone cost maximum.
- Completely centralized networks have access cost maximum/ backbone cost minimum.

Usually, our optimum scenario is somewhere in between these two extremes. We are searching for the more cost-effective WAN structure, so the cheapest combination of access, backbone, and hardware costs. At this point, our objective is just to identify the possible topologies. So we identify how many and where the backbone nodes are in each scenario, understanding scenario as the volume of traffic to make a backbone node feasible.

The aggregation nodes identification is made based on a predefined group of possible nodes (see chapter fourteen), distance, and traffic volume. We define the potential nodes, the distances are calculated based on the geodesic coordinates, and the volume is based on the traffic pattern of a typical traffic generator unit (workstation or people) and number of traffic generator units per traffic unit (site).

The identification of all possible topological scenarios is just the first step in the process of designing a WAN. The ideal WAN will be identified only when we test each possible topology considering all available interconnection costs.

15.1.1 The Process of Identifying the Topologies

Several algorithms are available to identify network topology. The algorithms to identify the aggregation nodes have the following as their objective: Given a group of possible nodes, identify the number and location of the nodes based on the minimum amount of traffic that would make a node justifiable. Center of mass (COM) algorithms and Sharma algorithms are examples of methods that can be used in this kind of analysis.

Basically, the process consists of calculating the distance between each traffic unit and all possible nodes. Then we verify the smaller distance and associate the volume of the traffic unit to the potential node. We repeat this procedure for all traffic units. When we finish this process, we verify the volume of traffic associated with each potential node. The potential nodes whose traffic volume equals or exceeds a given value are saved in this topology.

Then we vary the minimum volume of traffic to justify the existence of an aggregation node and repeat the procedure. We usually initiate the calculations defining the initial minimum volume and incremental volume. We typically define as the initial minimum volume the volume generated by the traffic generator unit. This process generates a range of topological scenarios From a completely distributed to a completely centralized topology.

In the end of this process, we have a file with all nodes identified considering all possible volumes (volumes to justify the existence of a node). The sequence of activities executed by these algorithms vary, but they are usually as follows:

1. Calculate the traffic load (in/out) of each traffic unit (site) based on the number of traffic generator units and in the traffic pattern.
2. Calculate the smaller distance between each traffic unit (site) and possible aggregation nodes (predefined) identifying the nearest aggregation node.
3. When finishing the distance calculations, verify how many traffic units were associated with each node and the total associated traffic.
4. Once we identified the traffic volume associated with each node, we verify if this volume equals or exceeds the volume of traffic defined as the minimum volume to justify a node. If the associated volume is smaller than the minimum, the node is eliminated as a potential aggregation node. The process is repeated until all nodes have a volume equal or superior to the defined minimum value.
5. When all nodes have a volume equal or superior to the minimum volume defined, save the topology, increment the minimum volume, and repeat the steps 2, 3, 4, and 5.

6. Repeat this process until the minimum volume to justify a node is equal to the total network traffic. Then we have all possible topologies.

15.1.2 The Traffic Volume Calculation of Each Traffic Unit

In this process, we apply the formulas discussed in chapter fourteen based on the number of traffic generator units (workstations or people in a corporate network) located in each traffic unit (site). The calculation of this load is crucial because the clustering process is based on distance and load. The aggregation node load in its turn is identified based on the sum of the loads of the traffic units associated with the node. Based on these calculations, we identify the traffic in/out of each aggregation node and build the data traffic matrix.

		21	11	512	246	123	852	482	922	192	244	612	473	912	152
21	RIO DE JANEIRO	26873	95604	46597	1941	804	3538	1978	3448	3083	652	7780	993	2603	392
11	SÃO PAULO	21148	578	2686	84	611	580	402	597	1267	5	1629	306	381	518
512	PORTO ALEGRE	24486	9797	32266	0	166	138	166	97	83	0	183	152	30	30
246	CABO FRIO	0	0	0	0	0	0	0	0	0	0	0	0	0	0
123	SÃO JOSE DOS CAMPOS	54	480	2	0	3	4	0	130	0	0	0	0	0	0
852	FORTALEZA	191	51	0	0	0	1	0	0	0	0	5	0	12	0
482	FLORIANOPOLIS	755	504	40	0	0	3	3	5	1	0	19	259	7	0
922	MANAUS	1359	1262	57	0	0	0	1	0	1	0	47	4	440	0
192	CAMPINAS	0	4	0	0	0	0	0	0	0	0	0	0	0	0
244	BARRA DO PIRAÍ	0	0	0	0	0	0	0	0	0	0	0	0	0	0
612	BRASILIA	1128	343	1	0	0	3	5	18	0	0	0	0	10	0
473	BLUMENAU	767	760	20	0	0	4	14	5	0	0	34	85	0	0
912	BELÉM	740	209	15	0	0	0	0	19	0	0	25	0	0	0
152	SOROCABA	3	0	0	0	0	0	0	0	0	0	0	0	0	0
732A	EUNÁPOLIS	0	0	0	0	0	0	0	0	0	0	0	0	0	0
383	SALINAS	0	0	0	0	0	0	0	0	0	0	0	0	0	0
422	PONTA GROSSA	0	0	0	0	0	0	0	0	0	0	0	0	0	0
242	PETRÓPOLIS	0	0	0	0	0	0	0	0	0	0	0	0	0	0
312	BELO HORIZONTE	4261	1869	6	4	0	0	0	22	3	0	286	0	0	0
712	SALVADOR	65	10	0	0	0	0	0	0	0	0	8	0	0	0
125	GUARATINGUETÁ	1	0	0	0	0	0	0	0	0	0	0	0	0	0
122	TAUBATE	5	0	0	0	0	0	0	0	0	0	0	0	0	0
243	VOLTA REDONDA	1	0	0	0	0	0	0	0	0	0	0	0	0	0
194	PIRACICABA	0	0	0	0	0	0	0	0	0	0	0	0	0	0
982	SÃO LUIS	1228	376	185	0	0	26	0	0	0	0	1	0	30	0
166	RIBEIRÃO PRETO	45	229	6	0	0	2	0	6	0	0	4	0	0	0
822	MACEIO	51	69	275	0	0	0	47	7	0	0	0	0	0	0
412	CURITIBA	10250	4356	1921	0	22	598	164	90	82	0	197	1019	83	14
326	ALEM PARAIBA	0	0	0	0	0	0	0	0	0	0	0	0	0	0
322	JUIZ DE FORA	1	0	0	0	0	0	0	0	0	0	0	0	0	0
812	RECIFE	80	19	0	0	0	14	0	15	0	0	4	0	0	0
382	MONTES CLAROS	0	0	0	0	0	0	0	0	0	0	0	0	0	0
792	ARACAJU	48	116	0	0	0	0	0	0	0	0	0	0	0	0
272	VITORIA	308	133	1	0	0	0	0	0	0	0	0	0	0	0
642	CAXIAS DO SUL	4	4	1	0	0	0	0	2	0	0	0	0	0	0
166	SÃO JOAQUIM DA BARRA	14	0	0	0	0	0	0	0	0	0	0	0	0	0
455	FOZ DO IGUAÇU	80	8	0	0	0	0	1	36	0	0	0	0	0	0
474	JOINVILLE	383	350	28	0	0	0	27	0	0	0	5	58	0	0
332	GOVERNADOR VALADARES	0	0	0	0	0	0	0	0	0	0	0	0	0	0
446	LOANDA	0	0	0	0	0	0	0	0	0	0	0	0	0	0
632	ARAGUAINA	456	149	8	0	0	0	4	0	0	0	125	0	71	0
442	MARINGA	34	0	52	0	0	0	1	64	0	0	0	0	0	0
452	CASCAVEL	0	0	0	0	0	0	0	0	0	0	0	0	0	0
842	NATAL	374	38	1	0	0	1	0	0	0	0	1	0	0	0
624	MORRINHOS	0	0	0	0	0	0	0	0	0	0	0	0	0	0
179	SÃO JOSE DO RIO PRETO	0	0	0	0	0	0	0	0	0	0	0	0	0	0
247	CAMPOS DOS GOYTACAZES	0	0	0	0	0	0	0	0	0	0	0	0	0	0
655	SINOP	0	0	0	0	0	0	0	0	0	0	0	0	0	0
926	BOA VISTA	34	175	12	0	0	0	0	76	0	0	7	0	46	0

Based on the flows (traffic matrix), we identify the necessary capacity of each connection for each combination of flows over physical routes. Two types of algorithms can solve this kind of problem: algorithms using continuous attribution or discrete attribution (serial merge).

15.1.3 The Process Governing the Elimination of Potential Nodes

The elimination of potential nodes when the associated volume is smaller than a given defined volume is not direct. We eliminate the potential nodes one by one. It has to be done in this way because, when we eliminate a node, the sites associated with it will be reassociated with other nodes, which may or may not already have the minimum necessary volume. Some nodes whose volume was not enough after the elimination of a node may become eligible.

So it is important to have proper node elimination criteria. Typically, we follow the sequence:

- Node with the smaller number of traffic units goes first
- Node with smaller traffic volume goes first (in or out)
- Node that is near to a survival node goes first

It is important to understand that several other criteria may be used, including arbitrary criteria linked with administrative aspects.

15.1.4 Clustering Curve

When continuing with the topology identification, we also identify the clustering curve, an interesting partial result that shows us the correlation between percentage of traffic generator units per distance range when we vary the number of aggregation nodes (topological scenarios). This curve gives a clear view about the organization's geographical dispersion. We usually adopt nine distance ranges.

Range number	Distance
0	X<=20km
1	20km<x<=50km
2	50km<x<=100km
3	100km<x<200km
4	200km<x<=300km
5	300km<x<500km
6	500km<x<=700km
7	700km<x<=1000km
8	x>1000km

Through this curve, we can clearly see how the percentage of traffic generator units (workstations, for instance) or traffic units (sites) per distance range vary when we vary the number of nodes (topology variation). This clearly shows how the increase or decrease of the number of nodes (topological scenarios) is influential in the organization's traffic distribution. In addition, this information helps to identify how far from ideal a structure may be without the need for a complete study.

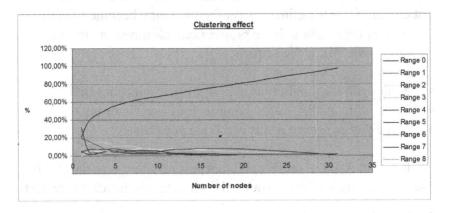

As we can clearly see, the Δ of variance of percent of sites in the closer ranges stops increasing at the same rate around seven nodes. That means the effectiveness of topological rearrangements starts decreasing.

Number of nodes	Range 0	Δ of variation of the number of nodes	Δ of variation of the number of workstations	Δ per node
1	21,10%			
2	39,78%	1	18,68%	18,68%
4	51,54%	2	11,76%	5,88%
5	56,18%	1	4,63%	4,63%
7	61,07%	2	4,89%	2,44%
8	62,83%	1	1,76%	1,76%
10	66,25%	2	3,42%	1,71%
12	69,38%	2	3,13%	1,56%
20	81,69%	8	12,32%	1,54%
31	97,17%	11	15,48%	1,41%

15.1.5 Topological Scenarios Generation

The results of this phase are all possible topologies, including the number and location of the aggregation nodes. Here we have all results of all elimination cycles (scenarios), understanding scenarios as the minimum amount of traffic, that make a node feasible.

15.2 *Analyzing the Alternatives*

It is initially important to understand that what is really going to define the ideal design is the interconnection costs (access and backbone). We know that, in general, the access costs tend to be inversely proportional to the number of aggregation nodes. In general, the more nodes we have, the cheaper the access tends to be. On the other hand, the more nodes we have, the more expensive the backbone hardware tends to be. Those tendencies are not absolute, and there are tariff systems where distance is not a relevant cost definition factor. In these environments, topology may not be as important, and the statements made before may not be true. From the analytical process point of view, a tariff system where distance is not a cost definition factor does not make any difference. In these environments, we usually tend to identify the best alternative as a star topology with the center of the star being the main data center.

In this phase, we identify the combination of backbone, access, and hardware that produces the smallest costs. This analysis is executed based on the possible topological scenarios. This process consists of calculating the costs to provide connectivity for each topological scenario using the available alternatives (service providers and technologies).

Our challenge is to identify which combinations (topologies and services) produce the cheaper designs. The identification of these designs usually happens through exhaustive search (verifying all possible scenarios). This calculation involves the following sequence for each scenario: backbone cost calculation, access cost calculation, and hardware cost calculation.

This determines the total cost for each scenario. This sequence demands preliminary calculations of node traffic volumes (based on the number of associated traffic generator units), traffic flows, and traffic matrixes (based on applications and their volumes). In other words, this happens for each scenario:

- Calculate the ideal backbone for this scenario (combination of flows, physical routes, and services):
  - Aggregation nodes traffic load calculation
  - Backbone flows identification
  - Identification of the available interconnections
  - Identification of the physical routes available

- Calculate the ideal access for the scenario
- Calculate the ideal hardware for the scenario

In summary, for each topology, we identify the ideal combination of flows flowing over the physical paths connecting the backbone nodes, calculate the ideal backbone cost (with all services alternatives available), and calculate the access and hardware costs. If our intention was to build a business case, we can also vary the traffic volume. In the end, we have an ideal WAN to a specific topological scenario. Repeating the process for all scenarios, we identify the ones with smaller costs.

The analysis encompasses four phases of calculation: flows calculations, backbone cost calculation, access cost calculation, and hardware cost calculation. Each step of analysis of the topology will be presented in the following sections. In the end, the goal of all of these calculations is to identify the ideal configuration.

15.2.1 Flows Calculations

Here we identify the flows among the aggregation nodes (traffic interest). This is based on the data and voice traffic matrixes of the traffic units (consolidated by nodes). Assuming applications generate traffic in/out, which is going to flow between the sites and the aggregation nodes and between the nodes themselves. At this point, the availability of physical interconnections to support the flows is not an issue. These flows will be combined over possible physical routes in order to identify the ideal backbone, that is, ideal in economical terms.

15.2.2 Backbone Cost Calculation

Here we are going to use abrangent trees determination with minimum restriction techniques (MST). The algorithms to determine such abrangent trees have as an objective the interconnection of the backbone nodes trying to minimize the number of connections (path length). The tree is called *abrangent* because it includes all aggregation nodes to a given topology.

In the MST logic, there is no limit to the number of nodes that the tree branches support. As an example of algorithms belonging to this class, we could mention Prim and Kruskal. To properly calculate a backbone in each topological scenario, it is necessary to follow the steps:

- For each topology, we analyze all possible physical routes.
- For each possible combination of routes, we analyze all possible combinations of application flows.
- For each possible combination of flows over routes, we test all possible service providers and all possible technologies available in each interconnection.
- Doing this, we find the optimum backbone cost.

In addition, as a byproduct, we execute all calculations and generate all the configuration logic of the equipment. Just to illustrate the complexity of the problem, let's assume a situation where we locked the topology into seven nodes, assuming a company with two data centers and six applications. We also assume that we are going to compare five service providers and each one has six alternatives of services. In this specific topology, we have:

- 6^6 possible physical routes = 46,656
- Six applications and two data centers
- Five service providers with six services each

- Number total of alternatives compared for this topology:
  $46,656 \times 6 \times 5 \times 6 = 8,398,080$

  Graphically, this situation can be represented as follows:

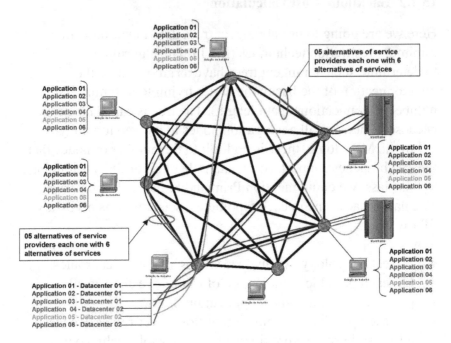

The number of alternatives analyzed grows enormously when the number of nodes grows:

- $4^4 \times 6 \times 5 \times 6 = 46,080$
- $5^5 \times 6 \times 5 \times 6 = 562,500$
- $6^6 \times 6 \times 5 \times 6 = 8,398,080$
- $7^7 \times 6 \times 5 \times 6 = 148,237,740$
- $8^8 \times 6 \times 5 \times 6 = 3,019,898,880$
- $9^9 \times 6 \times 5 \times 6 = 69,735,688,020$
- $10^{10} \times 6 \times 5 \times 6 = 1,800,000,000,000$

What would be the possibility to identify the ideal design if analyzing a backbone with ten nodes manually? What is the chance that the manually identified design is even among the best 10 percent? This example shows why we need tools to help us design

WANs properly and why designs made through these tools tend to be so much better and generate substantial savings.

If we take our example, for five service providers, each one offers six different services. Each one of these services may use different pricing strategies and demand different parameters to have their prices calculated (prices, total volume, bandwidth, distance, taxes, state boundaries, countries boundaries, CIRs, and so forth). Then we can clearly understand how difficult it would be to compare the alternatives.

15.2.2.1 Calculating the Physical Connections

At this point, we calculate all possible physical connections among the aggregation nodes and all possible routes. Here it becomes necessary to introduce constraints to limit the excessive number of physical connections. If no constraints were defined, the calculations will assume that all connections are feasible. A situation like that is not recommended because it generates an excessive number of possible routes overloading the computer executing the processing without adding value. As already mentioned in chapter fourteen, the inexistence of limitations in terms of physical connections is very rare.

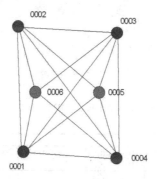

The backbone depicted in the picture above would have fourteen physical connections.

15.2.2.2 Calculating the Routes

In this phase, we calculate all possible routes interconnecting the aggregation nodes. Here there is also the need for limiting the number of hops to avoid an excessive number of possible routes. This means we are going to use algorithms, MST with hop restrictions. The algorithmic Esau-Williams and Sharma are two examples of MST with hop restrictions.

The algorithms to determine the minimum path have as an objective, given a predefined group of nodes, to identify the path whose length is minimal. We also can include the Bellman-Ford and Dijkstra algorithms in this class.

Consider a WAN with a defined topology and the traffic flows already known. Let's assume we want to identify the ideal voice flow and ideal structure. This is an optimization routing problem. The flow deviation algorithms and Bertsekas-Gallager algorithm are two possible methods that can be used to optimize this routing. This analytical process occurs in the following way. The previous example introduces some limitations in order to reduce the number of available physical connections.

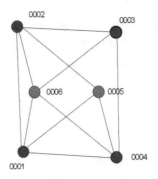

The available physical connections are:

Number	Connection	Number	Connection
1	0001 0002	7	0002 0006
2	0001 0004	8	0003 0004
3	0001 0005	9	0003 0006
4	0001 0006	10	0004 0006
5	0002 0003	11	0004 0005
6	0002 0005		

Based on the physical connections, we identify all possible routes linking each aggregation node to the data processing nodes. In this example, our traffic interest is concentrated into only two nodes: 005 and 006. We are not allowing flow through these two nodes. These are the routes available for a flow from node 0001 to node 0006:

Route	Sequency
1	0001 0006
2	0001 0002 0006
3	0001 0002 0003 0006
4	0001 0002 0003 0004 0006
5	0001 0004 0006
6	0001 0004 0003 0006
7	0001 0004 0003 0002 0006

Generating these routes for every node, we identify all possible routes. Here we should introduce constraints. No route can have more than three hops. In our example, if we adopt this criteria, the routes 4 and 7 would be discharged as alternatives. Using this criterion, we would have just five routes linking node 0001 to node 0006.

15.2.23 Identifying the Ideal Backbone

Now we have identified the routes and flows, we have to proceed the search to find which combination of flows over physical routes produce the least-cost backbone.

	Route	Sequence
	1	0001 0006
	2	0001 0002 0006
	3	0001 0002 0003 0006
Node 1	4	0001 0002 0003 0004 0006
	5	0001 0004 0006
	6	0001 0004 0003 0006
	7	0001 0004 0003 0002 0006
	Route	Sequence
	1	0002 0006
	2	0002 0001 0006
	3	0002 0001 0004 0006
Node 2	4	0002 0001 0004 0003 0006
	5	0002 0003 0006
	6	0002 0003 0004 0006
	7	0002 0003 0004 0001 0006
	Route	Sequence
	1	0003 0006
	2	0003 0002 0006
	3	0003 0002 0001 0006
Node 3	4	0003 0002 0001 0004 0006
	5	0003 0004 0006
	6	0003 0004 0001 0006
	7	0003 0004 0001 0002 0006
	Route	Sequence
	1	0004 0006
	2	0004 0001 0006
	3	0004 0001 0002 0006
Node 4	4	0004 0001 0002 0003 0006
	5	0004 0003 0006
	6	0004 0003 0002 0006
	7	0004 0003 0002 0001 0006

In this example, we have the flows flowing to and from only to two nodes (005 and 006). (In the picture above, we show only the routes going to node 006.) There is not any traffic interest among the nodes 0001, 0002, 0003, and 0004. We test all possible combinations of flows over the available physical routes. When doing that, we identify the demand (bandwidth) of each physical connection. Based on this demand, we calculate the cost if the link was contracted from every possible service of every service provider.

We usually have the possibility of setting the tool to, instead of calculating the ideal technology, service, or vendor in link-by-link or node-by-node basis, to do it by analyzing the alternatives as a whole. For instance, instead of showing which service provider is more cost-effective for each specific circuit, we would calculate which service provider could offer the cheaper solution to all circuits combined. In the same way, instead of showing which vendor has the best price for each node configuration, we can analyze which vendor can provide the more cost-effective proposal, assuming it would provide the services to all nodes. These kinds of verification would be virtually impossible manually. So we can continue the alternative selection using two possible strategies:

- **Per connection:** Selecting the smaller cost of each connection considering all available services and providers (connection-by-connection basis)
- **Per provider:** Selecting the smaller cost considering all connections contracted to only one provider (provider-by-provider basis)

15.2.3 Access Cost Calculation

Here we calculate the smaller access cost for each topology. In the same way as when calculating the backbone, we may use two different strategies:

- **Per connection:** Selecting the smaller cost of each connection considering all available services and providers (connection-by-connection basis)
- **Per provider:** Selecting the smaller cost considering all connections contracted to only one provider (provider-by-provider basis)

These calculations are executed by a family of software called interconnection cost calculators based on the parameters defining the costs (chapter fourteen).

15.2.4 Hardware Cost Calculation

Here we calculate the cost of the hardware associated with each node for each topology. Through this process, we identify the cost of each type of hardware available (being considered as alternative) (chapter fourteen) based on the traffic volume associated with the node. This volume can be traffic units (sites) or traffic generator units (workstations or people). We built the hardware calculators based on our typical node and on the alternative of hardware being considered. We must be able to establish the correlation between traffic volume and TCO of hardware, all referred to one month.

15.3 Identifying the Best Design

Once we have executed all calculations (backbone, access, and hardware) for each topological scenario and identified the ones that produce the smaller total cost, the designs must be compared. This problem is a heuristic problem, so it may encompass more than one possible solution. So the outcome of this final phase is the more cost-effective designs, including all details necessary to really implement it. Based on the best theoretical designs, we have now confronted them with the technical, administrative, and negotiable realities of the organization. Doing so, we refine the designs and identify the truly ideal one. Each alternative of design must encompass the following information:

- Backbone
  - All routes interconnecting each aggregation node
  - All flows among all aggregation nodes
  - Indication of all links (physical connections) used (point A and point B)
  - The bandwidth of each link used
  - The ideal technology to be used by each link
  - The ideal service provider for each link
  - The price of each link

- • The total backbone cost

- • Access
  - • Indication of all access circuits used (end A and end B)
  - • Each access circuit bandwidth
  - • Each access circuit technology
  - • Each access circuit service provider
  - • Each access circuit price
  - • Total access cost

- • Hardware
  - • Each node hardware cost
  - • Each node hardware vendor
  - • Total hardware cost

- • General information about the network
  - • Total network cost
  - • Number of sites (or traffic volume) that makes the node feasible
  - • Number of nodes identified in the optimal design

With this information, we have all necessary elements to really implement the network. Of course, we may perform adjustments, and commercial aspects may play their role as well.

16

Evaluating and Selecting Designs and Making Adjustments

Once we have calculated the best theoretical scenarios, we have to confront them with the practical realities of the organization to be able to effectively identify the ideal scenario(s). We initially have to verify the differences between the scenarios and the organization's actual structure. The objective is to verify which design(s) would demand less effort and smaller time to be implemented.

We also have to confront the designs with the contractual context of the organization, verifying which design would demand smaller costs of contract rearrangements (for example, avoiding penalties). Contractual penalties are relevant cost factors.

We also have to verify the compatibility with the existing hardware that the organization may own with the proposed designs. Although we usually consider the hardware costs when preparing the designs, if the organization already has its own hardware, it eliminates the need for this cost factor. So this possibility (using the existing hardware) must be considered. Having the possible designs, we will be particularly well equipped to negotiate with the service providers. Parameters used to prepare the designs may change due to these negotiations. It may be a back-and-forth process.

For instance, if just a small part of the circuits were recommended to be contracted with a given service provider (design generated by the design tool), it may make sense from the operational point of view to contract all circuits from the same provider as long we manage to negotiate the same prices of the cheapest alternative. In addition, having several design alternatives makes it possible to confront the service providers not only with smaller prices alternatives, but with different transport strategies. For example, if the value of the spoken minutes in the long-distance calls were not below x, we may use our private network where the cost is 0.8x. (We discuss the several aspects involved in a negotiation in chapter six.) At this point, we also have to decide about our backup strategy.

In summary, we are going to make adjustments contemplating technical, commercial, contractual, and strategic aspects. This phase could be divided into the following phases:

- Understanding the current situation
- Comparing the proposed designs with the contractual context
- Comparing the proposed designs with technical context
- Using the designs to negotiate
- Defining the backup strategy
- Redesigning the network
- Calculating the ROI

16.1 Understanding the Current Situation

Having a clear understanding of the current situation of the telecommunications infrastructure makes the team in charge of the project able to define which designs are really ideal in terms of cost, time, and implementation effort. In addition, having a clear view of the current situation makes it possible to compare the foreseen costs with the current ones. Having this information, we can see the project's ROI. When analyzing these structures, we normally manage to get substantive savings. During this process, we also identify which equipment needs to be replaced (upgraded) and identify the project's time frame. During the design process, we also can analyze strategic alternatives, such as outsourcing and external management.

16.2 Comparing the Proposed Designs with the Contractual Context

Each contract must be verified. Each contract's scope, time to termination, and penalties for early termination is applied to proposed designs. Through this verification, we must understand exactly the cost involved if we terminate each contract completely or if we reduce its scope. We must be able to see how this cost changes with the time (today, three months, six months, or a year). These values are crucial when calculating the ROI. The early termination penalties are usually quite significant. Designs that are closer to current reality may rate well at this phase. Major redesigns may cost a great deal more than calculated once termination fees are considered.

16.3 Comparing the Proposed Designs with the Technical Context

It is very important to understand how the network is physically/ technically structured. This understanding is very important because we have to know things such as if the equipment is bought or rented, if the equipment is old or up-to-date, and so forth. It is crucial to understand which limitations the hardware being used imposes to the structure. Hardware in this context does not mean only network hardware.

In addition, the technical understanding is crucial to make us able to see all operational aspects of the organization. We may see situations such as an optimal design pointing to a topology with nodes in different locations than the operational centers of the organization. In situations like that, it is very important to make the theoretical designs as compatible as possible with the operational context of the organization. If not possible, we have to consider the cost associated with the operational rearrangements in the cost of each scenario. Considering technical and operational realities as they apply to each calculated design will eliminate surprises during implementation.

16.4 Using the Designs to Negotiate

Another aspect to be considered is the fact that, having the theoretical designs, we can interact with the service providers, confronting them with different transport strategies. Although it may not be a typical procedure, it can be done and, in some cases, must be done. If we manage to attain some commercial advantage directly (getting a discount from the service provider that makes the implementation of a new structure pointless, for example), we may review the whole strategy.

16.5 Defining the Backup Strategy

When designing a WAN, we must define a backup strategy. A backup strategy allows us to define reaction capacity of the WAN. When designing a network, we must define what is supposed to happen when each one of its components fail. Of course, the level of reliability of a network depends on the kind of activity of each organization. The business side must be able to inform how much downtime does cost. This information is not always easily identifiable, but an honest effort must be done to identify it, because this cost will be the basis over which the several backup alternatives will be considered. The following are some examples of backup strategies:

- Each aggregation node will have at least two circuits: one primary and another secondary (backup).
- The ping-pong traffic will be considered high priority; bulk traffic and voice are low priority. In case of failure of the main circuit, the WAN switches block the voice and bulk traffic and start sending only the ping-pong traffic through the backup link. Voice starts going through the public network; bulk traffic starts using only the spare capacity of the backup circuit (if any).

Having defined the macro backup strategy, we still have to define aspects such as if the backups will be kept empty and only be activated in case of failure of the main link or if they will be used to transport other types of traffic (such as voice) or even as overflow alternative for the main link. A typical arrangement involves transporting voice through the backup links and, in case of failure, redirecting the priority traffic through the backup links and redirecting voice through the public network (as normal phone calls).

For instance, if we assume this arrangement, we will have to remove the voice traffic when designing the network. When finishing with the design of the network without voice, we do a new design, using only the voice traffic but removing the alternatives selected to the main design, as if we had two separate networks overlapping.

When describing the process described before, we usually remove as alternatives all connections belonging to the service providers chosen in the main design. Doing that, we force the backup circuits to be provided by a different service provider than the one supporting the main design.

On-use backup circuits tend to be more reliable than the just-in-need ones. A resource used only eventually will have a much bigger chance to be defective when you need it. Furthermore, if you are using the circuits that otherwise would be empty, you are also saving money (transporting voice, for instance) and keeping them monitored.

16.6 Redesigning the Network

Once we verify the current situation; understand the contractual, technical and negotiable context; and define the fail strategy, we should refeed the algorithms with the new inputs. Once we recalculate all the designs, we have the possible scenarios in their final form. They are no longer theoretical designs, but practical ones.

16.7 Calculating the ROI

Once we defined the best designs, we calculate the ROI of each one of them, considering not only the monthly operational cost but also the implementation costs including, but not being limited to consulting and specialized services, early termination penalties, negotiation costs, hardware renewal, migration costs, operational costs, management costs, and internal workforce. Once we have all these costs properly mapped for each design, we choose the one where all factors compound a best alternative for the organization.

We do not see the design tools as a panacea. It does not matter how good the tool is. The designs will be as good as the information used to feed the tool. In all cases, the human evaluation is a critical factor. In this sense, we could say that designing WANs is as much an art as it is a science. The design tools work as large calculators, which help the designers to do all required calculations quickly and precisely. It is a mistake to think they produce results by themselves. At the end of the day, the man evaluating the tool results and matching them against the contextual realities is going to find the adequate design.

17

Varying the Volumes and Building Dynamic Business Models

Although the identification of an ideal structure to support a given traffic volume is in itself interesting, the deployment of algorithms allows us to do more than just identify the optimized design for a defined traffic volume. Having tools that allow us to calculate these structures quickly opens up the possibility to make many calculations using several traffic volumes. Through these analyses, we can establish the correlation between volume and cost and associated revenue in a public network.

The possibility to set many volume scenarios is extremely useful because it allows us to see how the infrastructure cost changes depending on the volume transported. So we can produce a graphic correlating these values. For instance, if we are analyzing a large private network, it becomes possible to make simulations where we can see how the cost varies when we vary the transported volume. It allows us to identify in advance the impact of a new application in terms of WAN cost. It also becomes feasible to verify if a service provider proposal is better considering not only the current traffic volume, but also a future one.

In the same way, if we are analyzing a service provider infrastructure, we can identify the correlation of revenues per volume (or market share). Doing so, we can identify the correlation traffic volume versus infrastructure cost and traffic volume versus revenue. With this information, it becomes possible to identify the company cash flow, break-even point (minimum amount of traffic necessary to make a project feasible), ROI, and profitability per traffic volume.

In summary, we can build service provider business models and consequently see the limits of feasibility involved in each business initiative/alternative. This kind of planning is crucial when planning investments in service providers, allowing the investors to properly evaluate the risk involved in the endeavor. It also enables the simulation of different charging strategies, evaluating the impact on the revenue stream. Of course, the success or failure of an investment in a service provider has a lot to do with the quality of the implementation team. However, having a tool that allows the investors to see the different scenarios is extremely helpful.

18

Closing Words

We hope you have enjoyed reading the book and see that it proves useful as a reference guide in the future. We tried to consolidate large suites of information that we expect will help you when managing, planning, and negotiating your WAN. The layout of the book started with the concepts followed by negotiation topics to the administrative aspects and finalizing the book with more technical subjects. The appendix includes examples of computer programs for specific calculations for use as a practical reference when applying the techniques described in this book.

Many of the topics discussed demand some previous understanding from the reader. Many of the opinions expressed may be somewhat controversial in its interpretation by the authors. We do not expect you to agree with every opinion. Additionally, organizational realities may drive a politically based decision making process, discounting a logical approach. However, we made an honest effort to put the important factors up front and the reasoning behind them.

No organization does everything right. Perfection is god feature. We understand that and recognize that most telecommunications managers are often too busy just keeping the lights on. Nevertheless, having a clear view of the ideal situation is always important and provides a framework within which to work and measure progress in the right direction. Additionally, the information provided will hopefully enable people involved with the planning of WAN infrastructures to view their role in a more strategic perspective and understand the benefits of proper planning.

We know that, as any human endeavor, this book is not perfect. We are very open to criticism and suggestions that may help us to provide an improved second edition. We also know that many points deserve further development. Nevertheless, we hope to have achieved our goal to provide a useful tool through which the IT and telecommunications managers can improve their networks and save their companies money.

This book is an attempt to share our experiences that encompassed long professional careers in roles as telecommunications managers, IT managers, hardware vendor representatives, telco representatives, and independent consultants. We know that many of the topics covered in the book may be viewed from a different perspective, depending on which hat you are wearing. We took the perspective of the users/owners of the WANs and wrote this book mostly for them. The hardware vendors and telcos, however, may benefit from this book by improving their understanding of the challenges faced by their clients.

As networks expand in size, complexity of application transport, global scope, and business impact of network failures, this book increases in the value that it adds to the planning process of networks. The book does not attempt to be an operations guide. It has to be viewed in the context of the planning cycle of WANs.

Appendix: Programs for Specific Calculations

In this appendix, we give examples of specific codes mentioned throughout this book. First, we discuss the Erlang calculators, which are fundamental to calculate the number of channels to transport a given voice traffic. Second, we describe how the curve readers work and give a practical example of a code to execute this calculation. The curve readers are basic instruments when calculating the necessary bandwidth to transport a given flow. Third, we give an example of a code to calculate topological arrangements (distance based on coordinates). Finally, we give an example of an interconnection cost calculator. Those examples do not intend to exhaust the subject. Their objective is just to give the reader a practical view of this analytical software. Another important aspect is the fact that these software items, which we call *tools* throughout this book, usually work together and the results of one calculation may be used as the input for the other.

A.1 Erlang Calculators

Erlang is a nondimensional measurement unit used in traffic studies as a statistical measurement unit of traffic volume. The name "Erlang" comes from the Dane engineer, A.K. Erlang, a pioneer in the study of telephone traffic and in the study of what is known today as the *queue theory*. The traffic correspondent to 1 Erlang refers to only one resource (trunk) in continuous use for one hour. For instance, if a given site has two telephone lines and both are in continuous use, that means 2 Erlangs of traffic. In another example, a radio channel is occupied for thirty minutes during an hour. This supports 0.5 Erlangs of traffic.

So 1 Erlang can be considered as a utilization factor per unit of time. In the same line, 100 percent of use of one trunk means 1 Erlang; 100 percent of use of two trunks means 2 Erlangs. For example, if a total usage of mobile phones in a given area is 180 minutes, that represents 180/60, or 3 Erlangs. In general, if the average frequency of calls entering is λ per time unit and if the average retention of calls is h, the traffic in Erlangs (A) will be as follows: $A = \lambda h$.

This type of calculation defines if a system is over- or underdimensioned. For instance, if we measure a traffic for one hour (during peak time), we may use this measurement to define the number of active trunks in a E1 trunk. Here it is important to understand that the disparity between the number of Erlangs and number of necessary trunks to transport the traffic is because the calls have an uneven distribution along the time (one call finishing and another one initiating immediately). There is a range of different formulas to execute this calculation. We subsequently present the algorithms to calculate the necessary number of trunks based on denial of traffic (if the volume of calls exceeds a given availability of trunks and the caller receives a busy tone) and retention (the caller waits in line). Such strategies are known by the names Erlang B and C, respectively.

The algorithms described subsequently identify, based on a given traffic in Erlangs, the necessary number of trunks. This calculation has as its basic input the traffic expressed in Erlangs and QoS desired. The number of trunks necessary to support a given traffic can be calculated based on two premises:

- If the traffic exceeds the volume, it will be denied. (User receives a busy tone)
- By retention, the situation is where the user stays in line while waiting for the next available attendant.

A.1.1 Based on Denial of Services (Erlang B)

```
* PROGRAMA : ER1.PRG

* AUTOR : Luiz Augusto de Carvalho

* DATA : 22/02/88

* OBJETIVO : Procedures com a formula B de Erlang

*PROCEDURE PERDAERL

* SUBROTINA PARA CALCULO DA PERDA EM UMA ROTA

* COM ACESSIBILIDADE PLENA

* N = Numero de Circuitos

* A = Trafego oferecido

* B = Perda calculada

ERRO = 0.0001
*@ 06,01 clear to 25,119


N= erlan1

b=1

do while b>quality

A = erlan1

B = 1

I = 0

DO WHILE (I<N) .AND. (B>=ERRO)

I = I+1

X = A*B

B = X/(I+X)

*? I,n,x,b

* wait

* IF I = N - 1

* @ 13 , 10 SAY "B"

* @ 13 , 15 SAY B PICT '999.999999'
```

```
* @ 13 , 40 SAY A

* ENDIF

ENDDO

* @ 14 , 10 SAY "I = "

* @ 14 , 15 SAY I

* @ 15 , 10 SAY "B = "

* @ 15 , 15 SAY B

N=N+1

enddo


RETURN
```

A.1.2   Based on Call Retention (Erlang C)

```
* PROGRAM : ErlangC.prg

* WRITTEN BY: Luiz Augusto de Carvalho

* DATE : 03/07/2002

* OBJETIVE : Calculates number of trunks for Call-centers

*********************************************************************

erlan1= (tpeople*(tivr/100))*(((tcall*taverage)/21.2)*(ttcf/100))/60

target=15;agetime=240 && 240 seconds

for m = (erlan1+1) to (erlan1+100) step 1

u = erlan1

fatorialm=1

for t= 1 to m

fatorialm= t* fatorialm

endfor
```

```
soma=0

for k = 0 to (m-1)

fatorialk=1

for t= 1 to k

fatorialk = fatorialk * t

endfor

soma = soma+((u**k)/fatorialk)

endfor

p = u/m

parc1 = (1-p)*soma

parc2 = (u**m)/fatorialm

parc3 = parc1+parc2

top = (u**m)/fatorialm

csa = top/parc3

answer=csa*averagetime/(m*(1-p))

&&? m,u,answer

if target>answer

exit

endif

endfor

&&? m,u,answer,target,csa,"resultado final"

ttin = int(m)*ttcomp*1024

ttout= int(m)*ttcomp*1024

replace tin with (ttin)

replace tout with (ttout)

replace ftotvol with (ttotvol*tpeople)

endif
```

A.2 Curve Readers

These programs verify the links measurement files (the measurement curves) and identify the parameters such as ideal CIR; total flown bits along the time; total of spoken minutes; minimum, maximum, and average traffic by unit of time; and ideal bandwidth to transport the traffic. These programs are called curve readers because the link's traffic measurements are usually represented through curves correlating volume versus time. The curve readers analyze these curves. The basic idea is demonstrated in the graphic below:

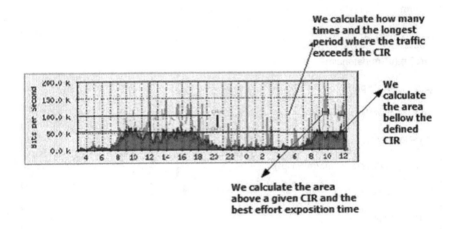

We calculate how many times and the longest period where the traffic exceeds the CIR

We calculate the area bellow the defined CIR

We calculate the area above a given CIR and the best effort exposition time

The whole idea is to vary the value of the bandwidth. Doing so, we will calculate which percentage of the traffic stays below this value. When doing this calculation, we also identify the total time during which the volume of traffic exceeds the defined value and the maximum continuous duration of these events (real traffic measured) exceeds the defined bandwidth traffic). We match the results (percent above the value, total duration of the time where the traffic exceeded the value, and maximum duration of the continuous time exceeding the value against a correlation of what the perception of the user is in the different technologies). Doing that, we identify what would be acceptable. If the defined value does not pass the test, we increase it by a given quantum and do the calculations again. We do that until we find a bandwidth that attends our demands in terms of QoS.

```
* PROGRAM : CURVEREADER.prg

* WRTTEN BY: Luiz Augusto de Carvalho

* DATE : 06/02/2002

* OBJETIVE : TRAFFIC CURVE INTEGRATION -DATA

***********************************************************************

use d:\prog\prog2\filex

go top

vol=0

do while .not. eof()

store n1 to tn1

store n2 to tn2

store n3 to tn3

skip

if .not. eof()

lateral= (n1*3600+n2*60)-(tn1*3600+tn2*60)

? n1,n2,tn1,tn2

if n3>tn3

high1= tn3

else

high1= n3

endif

high2=abs(n3-tn3)

area = (high1*lateral)+(high2*lateral/2)

vol=vol+area

* ? vol,area,high1,lateral,high2

* wait
```

```
endif

enddo

totalvol=vol

*wait

go top

store n1 to tn1

store n2 to tn2

go bottom

store n1 to ttn1

store n2 to ttn2

totaltime = (ttn1*3600+ttn2*60)-(tn1*3600+tn2*60)

average = vol/totaltime

maior = 0

go top

do while .not. eof()

tn3=n3

if tn3>maior

maior=tn3

endif

skip

enddo

? " average= ",average," maior= ",maior

wait

for valor = (average/2) to maior && Here we vary the possible value of our CIR and EIR

go top

vol=0

do while .not. eof()
```

```
store n1 to tn1

store n2 to tn2

tvalor1=n3

*? tvalor1,valor

if tvalor1>valor

tvalor1=valor

endif

skip

tvalor2=n3

*? tvalor2,valor

if tvalor2>valor

tvalor2=valor

endif

if .not. eof()

lateral= (n1*3600+n2*60)-(tn1*3600+tn2*60)

* ? tvalor1,tvalor2,valor

* wait

if tvalor2>tvalor1

high1= tvalor1

else

high1= tvalor2

endif

high2=abs(n3-tn3)

area = (high1*lateral)+(high2*lateral/2)

vol=vol+area

*? vol,area,high1,lateral,high2

*wait
```

```
endif

enddo


if vol>=(totalvol*.80) .and. vol<(totalvol*.82)

? totalvol,(totalvol*.80),vol,valor,average,maior

tcir = valor

* ? totalvol,vol,valor,average,maior

endif

if vol>=(totalvol*.95)

teir=valor

endif

endfor

nwork = 11 &&& We should define the number of workstations sampled

tcir = tcir/nwork

teir = teir/nwork

total= totalvol/nwork

? tcir,teir,total

** This program generates the recommended CIR and EIR of this application and the total amount of traffic per unit
```

A.3   Calculating Distance Based on Coordinates

This calculation is instrumental when defining the topology. Using these algorithms, we can calculate the distance of each site to the others identifying the centers of the gravity of the network. Of course, distance is not the only factor involved. The traffic load and adequacy to the existing public network are the other very usual decision factors.

```
DO WHILE .NOT. EOF()

tlatb = LAT

tlonb = LONg

ttmunicipio = NOME

tnode = numero

***********************************************

* CALCULO DA DISTANCIA *

***********************************************

pi=3.14159265

circunf=40077000

wy = tlona-tlonb

if (1296000-wy)<wy

wy=1296000-wy

endif

wy=((wy/3600))

w1=((((324000-tlatA)/3600)))

w2=((((324000-tlatB)/3600)))

w3=(cos(dtor(w2))*cos(dtor(w1)))+ (sin(dtor(w2))*sin(dtor(w1))*cos(dtor(wy)))

w4=(pi*.5)-asin(w3)

D=(circunf*w4)/(2*pi)

&& ? d,menor,ttmunicipio

if (D/1000) < MENOR

STORE (D/1000) TO MENOR

STORE TTMUNICIPIO TO TTT

STORE TNODE TO TTnode

STORE RECNO() TO TREC

if (MENOR < 5)
```

```
exit

endif

endif

skip

enddo
```

A.4   Interconnection Cost Calculators

Here we demonstrate an interconnection cost calculator based on discrete volume definition. In this particular case, given the volume and distance, we can calculate the cost of any connection. Note that each pricing strategy demands a specific code to be calculated.

```
* PROGRAM : PRICE.prg

* WRTTEN BY: Luiz Augusto de Carvalho

* DATE : 06/02/2002

* OBJETIVE : Interconnection cost calculator

*******************************************************************

**********************************************************************************

* Interconnection calculator based on EMBRATEL/WORLDCOM - BRAZIL prices *

**********************************************************************************

dimension tblnk(30,9) ;dimension tbvlr(30,9)


tblnk[01,01] = 14400 ;tbvlr[01,01] = 134.23

tblnk[01,02] = 14400 ;tbvlr[01,02] = 255.77

tblnk[01,03] = 14400 ;tbvlr[01,03] = 281.81

tblnk[01,04] = 14400 ;tbvlr[01,04] = 361.54

tblnk[01,05] = 14400 ;tbvlr[01,05] = 491.35

tblnk[01,06] = 14400 ;tbvlr[01,06] = 576.92

tblnk[01,07] = 14400 ;tbvlr[01,07] = 641.35
```

tblnk[01,08] = 14400 ;tbvlr[01,08] = 715.38

tblnk[01,09] = 14400 ;tbvlr[01,09] = 775.96

tblnk[02,01] = 19200 ;tbvlr[02,01] = 152.32

tblnk[02,02] = 19200 ;tbvlr[02,02] = 330.16

tblnk[02,03] = 19200 ;tbvlr[02,03] = 360.11

tblnk[02,04] = 19200 ;tbvlr[02,04] = 452.74

tblnk[02,05] = 19200 ;tbvlr[02,05] = 603.42

tblnk[02,06] = 19200 ;tbvlr[02,06] = 702.50

tblnk[02,07] = 19200 ;tbvlr[02,07] = 777.48

tblnk[02,08] = 19200 ;tbvlr[02,08] = 863.05

tblnk[02,09] = 19200 ;tbvlr[02,09] = 933.45

tblnk[03,01] = 28800 ;tbvlr[03,01] = 179.46

tblnk[03,02] = 28800 ;tbvlr[03,02] = 441.73

tblnk[03,03] = 28800 ;tbvlr[03,03] = 477.57

tblnk[03,04] = 28800 ;tbvlr[03,04] = 589.55

tblnk[03,05] = 28800 ;tbvlr[03,05] = 771.52

tblnk[03,06] = 28800 ;tbvlr[03,06] = 890.86

tblnk[03,07] = 28800 ;tbvlr[03,07] = 981.67

tblnk[03,08] = 28800 ;tbvlr[03,08] = 1084.55

tblnk[03,09] = 28800 ;tbvlr[03,09] = 1169.68

tblnk[04,01] = 38400 ;tbvlr[04,01] = 215.65

tblnk[04,02] = 38400 ;tbvlr[04,02] = 590.51

tblnk[04,03] = 38400 ;tbvlr[04,03] = 634.18

tblnk[04,04] = 38400 ;tbvlr[04,04] = 771.95

tblnk[04,05] = 38400 ;tbvlr[04,05] = 995.66

tblnk[04,06] = 38400 ;tbvlr[04,06] = 1142.00

tblnk[04,07] = 38400 ;tbvlr[04,07] = 1253.93

```
tblnk[04,08] = 38400 ;tbvlr[04,08] = 1379.89

tblnk[04,09] = 38400 ;tbvlr[04,09] = 1484.66

for var = 1 to 25

tbvlr[(var+4),1] = 275.96 + (var-1)*103.88

tbvlr[(var+4),2] = 838.46 + (var-1)*315.60

tbvlr[(var+4),3] = 895.19 + (var-1)*337.22

tbvlr[(var+4),4] = 1075.96 + (var-1)*405.33

tbvlr[(var+4),5] = 1369.23 + (var-1)*515.82

tbvlr[(var+4),6] = 1560.58 + (var-1)*588.15

tbvlr[(var+4),7] = 1707.69 + (var-1)*643.36

tbvlr[(var+4),8] = 1872.12 + (var-1)*705.49

tbvlr[(var+4),9] = 1009.62 + (var-1)*757.35

tblnk[(var+4),1] = 65536*var

tblnk[(var+4),2] = 65536*var

tblnk[(var+4),3] = 65536*var

tblnk[(var+4),4] = 65536*var

tblnk[(var+4),5] = 65536*var

tblnk[(var+4),6] = 65536*var

tblnk[(var+4),7] = 65536*var

tblnk[(var+4),8] = 65536*var

tblnk[(var+4),9] = 65536*var

endfor

FOR i = 2 TO 29

IF link[k1,k] =< tblnk[i,1]

*? "link ",link(k1,k),"tblnk ", tblnk(i)

EXIT

ENDIF
```

```
NEXT i

* ? i, degrau(k1,k)

tpreco=tbvlr(i, (degrau(k1,k)+1))


*? "tpreco",tpreco,"link ",link(k1,k)

*wait

* This routine based on the bandwidth and distance calculates the interconnection cost *
```

Bibliography

Ahuja, Ravindra K., Thomas L. Magnanti, and James B Orlin. *Network Flows Theory: Algorithms, and Applications.* Prentice Hall, 1993.

Ahuja. *Design and Analysis of Computer Communication Networks.* McGraw-Hill, 1982.

Barroso, Leônidas Conceição. *Cálculo Numérico.* Harper & Row do Brasil.

Bertsekas, Dimitri, and Robert Gallager. *Data Networks*, 2nd ed. Prentice Hall, 1992.

Black, Ulysses D. *Data Communications and Distributed Networks.* Reston.

Brosnan, Michael, and John Messina, and Ellen Block. *Telecommunications Expense Management.* Miller Freeman.

Cahn, Robert S. *Wide Area Network Design: Concepts and Tools for Optimization.* Morgan Kaufmann.

Daskin, Mark S. *Network and Discrete Location Models: Algorithms and Applications.* Wiley Inter-Science, 1995.

Dijkstra, E.W. 1959. A note on two problems in connection with graphs. *Numerische Mathematik* I:269–271.

Frank, and W. Chou. 1972. Topological optimization of computer networks. *Proceedings of the IEEE* 60:1385–1397.

Harnett, Donald L. *Statistical Analysis for Business and Economics.* Addison Wesley.

Kershenbaum, Aaron. *Telecommunications Network Design Algorithms.* McGraw-Hill in Computer Science Series, 1993.

Monma, C. L., and D.L. Sheng. 1986. Backbone network design and performance analysis: a methodology for packet switching networks. *IEEE J. Select Areas Communications* 4: 946–965.

Network Analysis Corporation, ARPANET. *Design, Operation, Management and Performance*. New York, April 1973.

Sharma, Roshan L. *Network Topology Optimization: The Art and Science of Network Design*. VNR Computer Library, 1990.

Software ARIETE. WANOPT.

Software TRMS Telecommunications Resources Management System. WANOPT.

Strother, S.C. *Telecommunications Cost Management*. Arthech House, 2002.

Wide Area Network Methodology. WANOPT.

Wrobel, Leo A. *Disaster Recovery Planning For Telecommunications*. Artech House.